Perchance

CONTENTS

CHAPTER vii

1 1

2 21

3 39

4 56

5 73

6 91

7 108

8 125

9 143

10 159

11 179

CONTENTS

12 | 198

13 | 212

14 | 234

15 | 257

ACKNOWLEDGEMENTS 261

Perchance

2 Cultures 2 Traumas 1 Dream

A Literary Romance by G. de Gwymbach

Indy Pub

She is standing on the beach just a stone's throw from the house where she has grown up. As she gazes at the horizon it seems to be opening.

It is coming.

Like a massive shadow in the distance at first, then the image starts to clear revealing a ship rushing towards her at incredible speed, much too fast. A great deal faster than would be realistically possible for its huge size. There is no doubt that it is going to hit the house.

Panicking, she calls for the mother who now appears, facing her, but some distance away. She tries to show the mother the gigantic ship, warning her that it will definitely hit the house. She crying out to the mother to help her, but the mother seems unable to hear, or understand, or to do anything. The huge ship is now just a breath away but only she can see it coming. Disaster is inevitable. She closes her eyes anticipating the moment of impact, the deafening noise of walls smashing, the dust cloud covering the sight of shapeless mountains of broken brick and fragments of furniture, the heaps of detritus, the smell of death.

There is no sound.

She opens her eyes. There is no sign of such destruction. The enormous ship has miraculously passed straight through the house, not bringing it down but opening a long, vertical slit in it.

She peers through the slit. In the lower part of the view she can see a dense forest, and a man who might be a shepherd, sitting under a tree. At his feet sit two deer, possibly tethered to the man, although there does not seem to be a rope. Perhaps not a physical link. The manner in which they sit at the man's feet seems unnatural. There is both attraction and unease within the tableaux for although it seems beautiful and serene there is a sense that all is not exactly pleasing or satisfying. There is just a hint of it being staged, furthermore the forest appears too dense and too dark.

She raises her eyes looking a bit higher. Now she can see her way out of the wood into a breathtaking scene, that of a vast, wonderful clear blue sky that is blissful, embracing. She is part of this bliss, this embrace, this one-ness that is spreading all over and into her, becoming part of her.

Her view changes. Two men are sitting on chairs that are placed at some distance from one another, with neither being too far away from her.

The first is a fairly young man, his thick hair is a deep black colour. She approaches him, trying to gain his attention or at least his acknowledgment of her presence, but the man keeps averting his eyes, as if looking for something or searching for somebody else.

The second man seems to be quietly, patiently waiting for her. He has lighter hair and is a little portly. He opens his arms to encompass her in a warm, soothing, loving embrace. She knows she has reached the place where she wants to be. It is as if she has at last found all that she might ever need.

1

Anna was playing with pleasure, this fantasy of hers invoking her husband, Panagiotis. She reveled in the wet kisses embellished with soft bites in their tender as well as passionate lovemaking, just as they had indulged themselves as a young, carefree couple. Her body was reacting to him now as it had done then some twenty years ago. Oh, how she needed him. She moaned, reacting to her intimate thoughts, her blood rushing, throbbing throughout her body.

The faint, clattering sound of her paintbrush hitting the floor brought Anna to herself with a start. Tiny splashes of red paint were flecked along her blue jeans, onto her trainers, and over the floor. Her palette was still resting in her left hand; thumb loosely emerging from it. Reality assured her that she was here, at home, in the room that served as her studio. Here she felt able to be her creative self despite the bleak outlook towards the flat roofs of the adjacent apartment blocks. The view of aerials, chimney pots, and lift cabins was hardly one to inspire artistic creativity, but that was entirely her own doing. "I need North light Panos" she had said to her husband, although to be truthful she only said so because it sounded 'artistic'. It did not seem to make any difference at all to the execution of her paintings and she wondered why on earth artists made such a thing about it. This workroom of hers, her studio, was therefor on the top floor at the back of their apartment where, due to the lack of proper roof insulation, it was cold in the winter and unbearably hot in the summer. The North Light wandered in from the large window, glancing off finished canvasses and 'work in progress' pieces, thereby seeming to mock her attempt at artistic acceptability.

Immediately in front of her stood her half-finished painting, the awakening kiss of 'Pygmalion and Galatea' depicting the moment when the sculptor brings his beautiful vision to life. She was determined to catch the essence of this scene, that showed allegorically such an important instant for any sculptor or painter. For it was just at this point that her artistic, creative dream emerged as a physical reality. How typical, she thought, that this beautiful myth of her own country, Greece, was only known nowadays because it was popularized by Ovid, a Roman. This country of hers was indisputably the source of so much creativity in the arts, architecture, theatre, philosophy and music, but this was negated by the absence of organization. Thus it had been two thousand years ago, and thus, she thought, it is now.

Panos had not overtly discouraged her artistic efforts although he was apt to make disparaging remarks about her ability. At least he had never tried to stop her. Her painting had become such an important part of her life, allowing her to express her feelings, her hopes and her delights. She now had good contacts with two galleries here in Athens where it seemed that her work was appreciated, and more to the point was sellable. Her style was classical rather than modern for unless you were a very well-known artist it was difficult to sell anything later that Impressionism. She did not make much money from these sales so she supplemented her income by doing some consultancy work on interior design with a very able real estate agent.

The last twinges of her fantasy tugged at her mind causing her to tremble at the vividness of her imagination; it was such a stark expression of need. But she knew better than to comprehensively lose touch with the real world. She would put this daydreaming behind her.

The actual, corporeal, Panos was, nowadays, hardly ever with her here in their Athens home, and sadly she had to accept that their lovemaking had deteriorated in recent years. In truth Panos' interested in sex had dwindled to the extent that his sexual technique was not half as skilful as the wonderful intimate scenes that she seemed to imagine so easily. It was almost as if Panos did not have the time or the need to show any kind of desire or tender emotion. Whilst he was prepared to perform adequately enough when required, he failed to bring to her the passion that she in her turn was so eager to express.

She longed for her 'old Panos', who really loved her. But perhaps this heightened sexual desire of hers was not really a longing for him, but rather a more carnal desire that was heightened by disassociating itself from her husband. No, she loved him. She just found it galling to have to accept the sad reality that he placed love for his job above any love that he might now feel for her. She was unhappy that he worked such long hours and that his job as a civil engineer took him away from her all week and every week.

"It'll only be for a short while darling" he had said when he accepted the promotion to Supervising Manager in the big firm where he was employed. "If I go on working hard and continue to do well then the next promotion will come along within a couple of years and we can buy that cruising yacht we have set our hearts on." Panos did indeed work hard, but the expected promotion never came and, slightly to her relief, neither did the boat.

She caught sight of the clock outside the studio door. She must be out of her mind. It was almost half past nine. The smell of sweat, mingling with that of turpentine, pervaded her body. Her clothes were splattered with paint and she, this unkempt artist, was not the person that she wanted to be to welcome home her hard-working man. Panos would be arriving at any moment now and she needed to make herself presentable, both for herself and for him. He would never acknowledge that she had established herself as a professional artist and made it clear that her primary role was that of a loving, caring wife. She had to pretend that painting to her was just an amusing hobby

From the kitchen there issued the wonderful smell of the meal she had so lovingly started to create earlier in the afternoon. She had prepared the chicken quarters and blanched the bacon to remove some of its saltiness. She had added onions, mushrooms some herbs out of her garden, and of course, some red wine. The meal was now simmering gently on the stove. There was true delight in being able to cook this dish that Panos enjoyed so much. Flavouring the fridge was a bottle of Santorini Atheri, Panos' favourite wine. In contrast to her, he had a clear preference for white wine, although admittedly it was a slightly strange choice for this meal.

Unlike the bathroom in many Greek apartments theirs had an outside window. She had spent a little time in England before they were married and had insisted that their bathroom should be like those she had experienced abroad. She stripped off her messy clothes, leaving them in a heap on the floor, and stepped into the shower. Over the years she had taken care of her body. She was slightly on the short side at 165cm and was slim without being thin. Her dark brown hair fell well below her shoulders and her skin, although naturally pale for a Greek, turned a light golden brown in the summer months.

It was a shame that this could not be a more leisurely shower, but such indulgence had been thwarted by over-involvement with that painting and then being carried away into a fantasy world. It had only been a daydream, but a quivering within her testified to the underlying reality of her desire.

She reveled in the water cascading through her hair, across her face and then sluicing over her lower body. Her hands felt downwards, running over her flat stomach.

"I want a baby just as much as you do, my darling," Panos had told her, "But I really have a responsibility to you and to our future child to ensure we are in a stable and comfortable financial position. Anyway, once I have that promotion, I will be able to devote so much more time to being a really good father."

She had believed him, although her body cried out that time was not on her side and she should have a baby right now.

Anna stepped out of the shower. She decided against turning on the air conditioning although a little of the heat of the day still lingered into this the Athens evening. The lightest of toweling ensured the continuance of the cool moist feeling over her body for a little longer.

The flowery patterned silk-cotton dress was a piece of cloth so light that it rippled at her slightest move, bringing with it both comfort and elegance. She gazed at herself in the mirror for a while, looking at her reflection. The thin fabric of her dress exposed much of her slim legs, the upper part of her breasts, and all of her shoulders and arms. For a moment she fancied that beyond this solid sheet of mirrored glass she caught sight of another Anna, the Anna that she should have become, who was properly recognized and loved.

"Can you never stop fantasizing today?" She laughed.

Music always succeeded in relaxing her, ridding her of the tension that was inside her. She should be playing a CD, it would make for a warmer, more welcoming, atmosphere when Panos arrived. She started to flip through the CDs as she sat on the arm of the woodcut Byzantine-style, hand-made sofa, a piece of the finest craftsmanship and Anna's most prized possession in all the house.

It looked as innocent as the day she both physically and mentally, against her husband's wishes, manoeuvred it into the apartment, absolving itself from responsibility for any part in the huge argument that it had engendered between her and Panos

"Jesus, Anna, this is way too expensive and much too uncomfortable!" he exclaimed indignantly. Panos had little appreciation of art, or indeed fine craftsmanship. His was a more practical turn of mind. A sofa should be all that a sofa needed to be: spacious, soft, and hospitable to the user. They already possessed one such. "Why on earth should I buy a second sofa that I'm never going to sit on?"

She could not come up with anything other than the rather feeble truth. "Just for the beauty of it." That had, of course, hardly convinced Panos, so she had to resort to other means, emotional blackmail based upon another truth.

"I never wanted this promotion of yours."

"It's for your benefit too, you know."

"I hate your long absences from home. I feel lonely and unloved in this empty place."

"It won't be forever."

"Look, I've put up with you saying that we should not have a child yet. Have you any idea what this is doing to me? How much I want a child? I need a child. We need a child."

She had finally got her child-substitute. She eyed it now as if it were an alien object from a parallel universe.

Panos should have been home at least half an hour ago. Given her tardiness it was fortunate that he was running a little late. His flight had been due to land at quarter past nine and it would not normally take more than thirty or forty minutes to drive from the airport at this time of the evening. But perhaps the plane had been delayed as so often they were, or he had become stuck behind one of those blasted dust-carts that the city-council seemed to organize so that they caused traffic chaos at the most impossible hours of the day or night.

Nevertheless time was passing and her lovingly prepared meal would not keep forever. Perhaps it would be a good idea to call his mobile? She was reluctant to do this except in some sort of emergency. At home he only used his mobile sparingly, complaining that during the working day he had it constantly pressed to his ear so that surely it would be frying his brain. That was fair enough. She could understand and did not expect him to phone her and thought it best not to call him.

She thought of ringing his hotel in Crete, just to be sure that he had not had to delay his return, but it would be unlikely that she would get much information from there.

On the few occasions that she had tried to phone him at the hotel the receptionist would come up with some excuse for not putting her through, either the line was busy, or else "Mr. Dimitriou has not answered the call." An enquiry as to whether he was in, would always fail to elicit a helpful response. "I regret to inform you that providing information as to the whereabouts of our customers is contrary to company policy." It was hardly helpful.

The landline phone rang, its strident tone breaking the silence of the house and jolting Anna out of her thoughts.

It rang again, just as intrusively, then a third time. It could only be Panos, but if he were ringing home at this time then he really was going to be very late. He must have some sort of problem,

The phone was ringing again and she rushed to grab it before she missed the call.

"Hello, Darling . . ." out of breath she managed to pick up the receiver. The voice at the other end of the line was that of a man she did not recognize.

"Good evening.... may I speak to Mrs. Dimitriou please, that is the wife of Mr. Panagiotis Dimitriou?" The voice, measured, a little dreary perhaps, contained just a slight fluctuation in tone that provided a softening effect upon its distant formality.

A numbness rose rapidly through Anna's body, starting from her toes and now arriving at her head. "You're speaking to her," she answered trying to concentrate so she would understand what this caller was trying to say to her.

There was a momentary hesitation whilst the man cleared his throat, this being either the affliction of a heavy smoker, or due to unease about what needed to be said. An overwhelming feeling of anxiety expanded within her and became part of her, a frozen block of ice where her stomach, and her heart, had once been. The man, who introduced himself as a policeman, was talking fast, as if he wanted to get this message out of him as quickly as he could. Her ears burned and her mind refused to register what was being said. This voice spoke so close to her ear and yet, it was as if it were from another world, a place with which she had no possible connection.

Things were being spoken that were unthinkable, a rumble of sound that she would have rejected as incomprehensible had it not contained a message so clear and simple and brief. Her husband had lost his fight for life in the AHEPA General Hospital in Thessaloniki, following a severe car crash on the National Road. She was required to visit the hospital for the formal identification of his body and the completion of the standard procedures....

A deafening buzzing in her ears prevented her from hearing anything further. She restrained herself from squeezing her temples to keep her head from exploding. This had to be some form of practical joke. There could be no truth in what was being said. The words kept ringing in her ears. Thessaloniki. National Road. General Hospital. Accident.

"Wait a minute. I'm afraid there must have been some misunderstanding." She tried to regain some composure, clutching at just one final life raft of hope. "My husband has had nothing to do with Thessaloniki or the National Road for at least four years now. He has just come off a flight returning from Crete. By now he will have landed at Eleftherios Venizelos airport. He should have been home by now. I'm expecting him to walk in the door at any minute …"

Her voice faded as the man interrupted her, firmly but kindly re-stating the facts. "I'm afraid that unfortunately there's no misunderstanding, Mrs. Dimitriou. We have your name and number, amongst others, from the mobile phone that he was carrying." Then he added mildly but not abandoning the formality that both the occasion, and his position, required, "May I take this opportunity to offer my sincere condolences."

His mission completed he rang off.

The phone was a dead thing in Anna's hand. For seconds it seemed as if it were glued there, as if some massive force was compelling her to hold it to her ear. Perhaps the arrow of time might go into reverse. This film would rewind and the person at the other end of the phone might be someone else, and would say something completely different.

Anna hung up the phone.

The Byzantine sofa appeared as solid as it had been when she had stood up from it those two lifetime-minutes ago.

The balcony door stood open and the buzzing, high-pitched sound of an electronic alarm clock forced its way into the room from an adjoining apartment. A dog barked in a neighbouring yard, and from the street below came the merciless shriek of a motorcycle being raced along a narrow alleyway. Such were the sounds of normality. The sounds of a life, her life, a life that had been hers, once upon a time.

Anna stood frozen, numb to the world. Her world. Her world that was disintegrating even as she stood there.

(Thessaloniki, Greece)

Glaring rays of fierce sunlight attacked Anna's exposed, red and swollen eyes almost blinding her as she emerged from the hospital in Thessaloniki. A frantic search of her handbag failed to reveal her dark brown sunglasses. They were not there, nor in the small bag of hand luggage. Why did she always find the most awkward situations to lose her sunglasses? Yes, she had them when she disembarked from the plane. Were they still with her when she arrived at the hospital or had she left them in the taxi? Perhaps she had left them somewhere in the hospital. If so, where? There were too many possibilities, perhaps at the reception desk, or the coffee table in front of the filthy bench where she had sat waiting.

Or could they be in the morgue? That word was stomach churning. Gross images from the awful place flooded into her mind. Oh, how awful to see that body, broken and twisted by the accident. They had done their best to make Panos' remains look presentable, but could not totally conceal the trauma that he had suffered.

The sunglasses must be in her bag. She bent down to peer in it, fumbling amongst its contents, glasses case, wallet, lipstick, handkerchief, phone, documents, receipts and an extra dark-blue summer dress that she had stuffed in there 'just in case'. As she bent down something flopped off her head and over her dark hair that, under the dazzling sun, seemed to be making an attempt to turn blond. The glasses fell onto the ground in front of her.

She was due to meet a woman who had contacted her only yesterday, a stranger who called herself Stella. The phone in the sitting room had rung a few times and then stopped. Anna was reluctant to answer, the last thing she wanted was to listen to stuttering condolences from friends, family, or business acquaintances. Half a minute later the phone started again, insistent, demanding. Anna reluctantly picked it up.

"Yes?"

"Am I speaking to Mrs. Anna Dimitriou?" This was a woman's voice, and one that she did not recognize.

"My name is Stella. You don't know me, but I have some information for you regarding your husband who was so tragically killed yesterday."

Anna said nothing. What could this all be about?

"I assume you are coming to Thessaloniki in the next day or so. May we meet, I really think it is in your interest that we should."

"I suppose so" Anna said." She took Stella's number and said she would phone her.

She had contacted this somewhat mysterious Stella as soon as she had landed and agreed to meet for coffee at Baraka, a café/bar in the centre of town. She had no idea what this woman wanted and hardly felt up to any sort of social contact. However Stella had been insistent that they should meet so she had taken a taxi to Tsimiski and walked up Dimitrou Gounari.

A tall, 30-something woman rose from one of the outside tables and held out her hand. "Hello, I'm Stella". She was undeniably attractive in the manner of a model, with long legs and a thin body. Her light brown hair was styled in a pixie cut. Despite her looks she did not appear to be in much better shape than Anna, Clearly she had been crying recently although she had made an attempt to cover her red and swollen eyes with concealer.

"I am in no condition for small-talk," said Anna, "tell me why you have contacted me at this unhappy time, and I will be on my way."

Stella was clearly nervous, fiddling with her coffee spoon and playing with her paper napkin. She was reluctant to meet Anna's gaze. "I really don't know how to tell you this," she said "I know it is going to be an awful shock to you. It will not be easy for you to understand and accept, but I would ask you, please, to try and remain calm and not judge me too harshly."

What could this information be that was so distressing that it would be difficult for her to take in? Anna was prepared for almost anything. Her chest fluttered with anxiety and her heart was responding with irregular beats. She waited with a growing unease.

"Anna," continued Stella, "this is really not easy for me to say, but by now you know that your husband was not on that flight from Crete that you expected him to have caught. I have known him for about four years and am fairly certain he had never been there during that time. You see for the larger part of each month, that is when he was not with you, Panagiotis worked and lived here, in Thessaloniki". She paused and searched for Anna's reaction.

Anna just stared at her expressionless. Her heart was pounding madly now.

"What I am certain you did not know was that Panagiotis was also committed here. By which I mean that we own a house and have two children, my son who is just three and my little girl who is one and a half."

Anna said nothing. Her whole world was spinning and she could not stop it. She made to stand up, but was overwhelmed. Her legs buckled beneath her and she slid to the ground, knocking over the chair and a glass of water. She was still half-conscious, but could not move her legs or arms. Far away she heard a waitress shouting,

"Kosta, call an ambulance. Now."

The café staff fussed around her for several minutes. It was overwhelmingly embarrassing to realise what had happened and Anna was even more, unhappy, angry and lost, when Stella's words returned, lingering in her head, like a half-remembered nightmare that was impinging on consciousness. It all seemed so unreal.

A number of worried faces were gathered around, observing, giving water, moistening her face, smiling with sympathy, and asking concerned questions. Was she all right now? Was there something they could do? If only they would go away and leave her. Someone took her pulse and suggested that perhaps she should be taken to hospital for a check-up.

"No, no hospital," she said, "and no ambulance. I'm fine". All she wanted now was a taxi to take her to the airport where she had a flight to catch.

"I am so sorry," said Stella. "This really shouldn't have happened."

Anna said nothing, wondering why this woman was still with her, perhaps gloating over her discomfort.

"I can imagine how difficult this must be for you, and believe me, I'm in a terrible condition myself," Stella was being kind rather than aggressive, but Anna was losing her patience. She had been maltreated enough for one day and did not want to talk to this imposter.

"What the hell to you want of me? Haven't you taken enough from me already."

"The only thing that I want is to be at Panagiotis' funeral. My children have a right to be there. Panagiotis was their father. I can well understand how upsetting our presence is likely to be to you, but it's important to us that we should be there."

Anna could not feel anything. However hard she searched there was no hurt, no anger, no disgust, indeed nothing at all to remind her that she was still human and very much alive. There was not one single emotion to be found. In the end, she came up just one question, asked out of curiosity. "You knew about me the whole time?"

"Yes," the woman answered.

So the dirty stinking sub-human rat who had been her husband had led a full open and honest life with this awful woman who was trying to be kind to her

She paused for a few seconds. "Very well, you can do as you like about the funeral, it is no concern of mine".

During the drive through the roads of Thessaloniki to the airport, and later as she looked vaguely out of the aeroplane window at nothing in particular, she tried to overcome the overwhelming swirl of feelings that were besetting her. It seemed as if betrayal and pain, rage and despair, were all trying to shoulder each other out of the way in competition for the exclusive occupation of her mind.

She needed to think in practical terms. It had been arranged that Panos' body would be transferred to Athens the next morning. There were the funeral arrangements to take care of and she had to let relatives know. Dora, Panos' mother, had moved to the States as soon as her husband had died, in order to be with her elder son, Petros. Anna had never liked his mother and apparently this feeling was mutual. They had not overcome their suspicion of each other, never really relaxing in their rivalry for primacy in Panos' heart. It was so ironic that in the end neither of them had won that.

Then there were his friends. Not many of them either. With his frequent long absences and lack of interest in maintaining contact, most of the people he had known eventually slipped out of his life. Perhaps she should call Kostas and Paulos who had remained faithful.

On her side - oh my, that was the toughest part – there were her parents, both in their seventies. How much should she tell them? Just learning the news of Panos' death would be enough for her father to need extra pills for heart and blood pressure, and surely mum would need an extra dose of her sedative? Telling them the whole truth about his second family would be so much worse; indeed she feared that it would finish them off. Clearly it would be irresponsible of her to tell them so much, so she would also have to construct a convincing excuse for not expecting her parents to attend the funeral. This was not going to be at all easy.

The plump middle-aged woman on the next seat, who had fallen asleep almost immediately after take-off, was now snoring rather loudly. Her flabby body was occupying the whole of her allocated space and she was, probably in search of some comfort, now leaning seriously to the right. Her head was lolling from time to time onto Anna's shoulder and, as the woman breathed heavily, her head moved in sync with the rhythmical movement of her ample chest. Anna wondered if she could push her back in place without waking her, but this mountain of a woman was far beyond Anna's weight-lifting prowess. She prodded her arm gently, then more persistently. The lady woke up with a jolt, looked first at Anna's shoulder, then in some surprise at Anna's face. Under different circumstances Anna would have smiled at the woman, perhaps she would have made a pleasant or witty comment, but just now such niceties were beyond her. She must have given her a rather stern glare for the woman smiled timidly and mumbled an embarrassed "I'm sorry". Five minutes later she had fallen asleep again, quickly resuming her previous position. Anna sighed.

Then there was her brother Lukas, just thirty now, nearly a whole decade younger than her, but with him at least she should not have a problem. Lukas was so open-minded and understanding, and yet, she knew he would regret that her 'bloody fraud of a husband' - she could just hear Lukas saying that - was not alive so he could have it out with him man to man. But Lukas would not burden her with inquisition and blame. Who else was there? Ellie of course; Ellie was three years younger and almost like a sister, her closest and perhaps only, true friend. The two of them had laughed when Ellie had graduated from law school at about the same time that she was marrying Panos. "I hope it'll never be necessary," Ellie had said with a smile, "but in case by any chance you need a divorce lawyer, you've got one here for free, lucky you." Ellie had said it in jest, but now Anna knew she would now need both Ellie's friendship and her professional expertise.

(Athens, Greece)

As she entered her house Anna experienced an intense urge to vomit. She ran to the bathroom and was sick. She relieved herself, and poured water over her face. She took off all her clothes but instead of putting them in the washing machine or in the laundry basket, she wrapped them up in a ball and tossed them into the rubbish bin with a swift, somewhat exaggerated movement. It was as if there would never be a detergent strong enough to clean those clothes and by the act of throwing them out into the rubbish she was ridding herself of all the pain and all the shame that was inside her.

Emerging from the bathroom she heard the house phone ringing, not her mobile. Her experience of the last calls she had taken on it presaged something equally unpleasant. She hesitated. Perhaps she should ignore it? But it might be her parents; they always called her on the home phone. She was uncertain as to whether she was ready to talk to anybody.

"Hello," said Stella, "I hope you don't mind. I'm just checking to see if you are okay."

"Fuck off." With a growing sense of injustice and cold rage Anna reached down and tore the phone cable from the wall, hurling the phone across the room.

So this was what it had all come to. She looked around the house, so quiet, so empty. This was her life, or what her life had been. These walls, these floors, this furniture had that been her companions. They had given her comfort and provided her with a sense of belonging. They had held the warmth of bodies; they exuded memories, laughter, words of love, promises full of hope, and smells of homemade gourmet food accompanied by glasses of wine. They had also held the loneliness and the anticipation and the failure and the anger and the apathy and the compromises that she had made.

She looked around the house as if she was searching for, inspecting, acknowledging the whole of the life she had lived here. Every single centimetre of the house, every piece of furniture and decoration, even every appliance, cried out with some personal memory. The expensive Bokhara carpet that she and Panos had made love on, bought as soon as they had moved into the house before they even had a sofa. The television set they had watched Kieślowski's Three Colours Trilogy, ever playfully disputing as to which was the best one of the three. The portrait she had given him as a birthday present. The poster, made out of a picture Panos had once taken of her whilst she was sleeping; the blender where she would mix peppermint, rum, sugar, lime and soda to make a Mojito cocktail for moments of festivity and mirth; the closet containing his clothes - and hers. All neatly washed and ironed, fragranced and softened with the best softener she had been able to find in the market. Their bed, that had been host to their hungry explorations, affectionate cuddling, and tired nesting - but also her own bed, her companion and comforter in nights of loneliness, when she had fumbled in the sheets for the memory of the warmth of a body that was absent, where she had smelled the pillows for a lingering scent in wet, fulfilling, promising dreams - and which had also featured in her nightmares.

It started slowly and rather quietly, without any sense of celebration. She pulled the sheets off the bed and flung them onto the floor. She took the pillowcases off and tossed them randomly around the room. One landed on the radiator, the other got stuck and hung on the copper leaves of the small bedroom candelabra. She started taking clothes out and throwing them on the floor, his clothes and hers. She eyed the bookcase and, with admirable strength, swept all the shelves from top to bottom. The books fell, ending up arranged like a heap of irregular crazed dominoes. She smashed the T.V. with the antique vase they had so longed to acquire, and with her own bare hands broke the glass cover of the poster of her as a sleeping beauty. She cut herself badly and blood spilled over the glass, the poster, and the wall with some of it slowly running down her arm.

She spat on the Bokhara and as her frantic steps took her from room to room she ended up in her studio. She looked at the 'Pygmalion' painting temporarily undecided. Finally she calmly approached it and after she had taken it off the easel, she thrust her foot through it, pulled it out and then thrust it in again, and again, and again, until the painting was turned into a rag of coloured canvas stripes surrounding the holes she had made, and hanging in all directions. When she was finished, and as if such treatment was not enough, she took the remains of the painting out onto the balcony and sent the tattered ghost of 'Pygmalion and Galatea' spinning in free fall from the fourth-floor apartment. This was not her home anymore. Neither had it been her life. She had not been living.

She fell asleep on the studio floor amongst the blood and tears and mucus.

2

(Lancaster, seven months later)

"And the winner of this year's Caesar Charleston prize for the best debut Romantic poet is . . ."

The ballroom of the Grand Hotel was oppressively hot. It was oppressively furnished; in fact it was oppressively everything. Presumably in its hey-day, in the era of the *thé dansant*, things had been different. An orchestra would have been playing serenely in the background, palms would have been gently waving in the lightest of breezes, guests would have been gliding easily between tables before taking to the renowned dance floor. But that had all been a long time ago, in a different world.

This evening the ballroom of the Grand had been given over to a private function. Every year the hospitality and tourism industries joined with their trading and manufacturing counterparts to be judged and duly rewarded by The Northern Business Initiative. Such a prize was hardly national news, but nevertheless it was recognition, most especially for 'up and coming' organisations. As the prize-giving progressed a sense of ennui prevailed, only alleviated by a decent quantity of alcohol.

The Master of Ceremonies was trying, in vain, to revive the flagging interest of the assembly. Eventually all the business prizes had been thrust into the sweaty hands of falsely smiling chairmen who, because their firms all contributed towards swelling the coffers of the NBI, were in effect awarding themselves large cheques for their achievements.

The MC was not quite done yet. This year, for the first time, the organising committee had decided that they should introduce something a little out of the ordinary. Thus this year there was a Poetry Prize. It was an anomalous little cultural postscript to an evening of lavish entertainment but the MC was spinning out his announcement of the winner as if he was hosting a major celebrity TV show. "Now, Gentlemen, and Ladies of course, it is time to celebrate a little bit of culture – eh? You keep the wheels of business turning but where would we all be without a bit of art – eh? We all need a bit of titillation – eh?"

'Eh - indeed' thought Nigel. What the hell was he doing here, an intellectual hostage amongst these thrusting, shiny-suited seekers after power? Admittedly his table seated half a dozen fellow poets, mostly with their partners, but even they seemed to be caught up in the overwhelming commercial spirit of the evening, one rather over-enthusiastic purveyor of doggerel even venturing to suggest that he was so enthused by the evening that he would be seeking sponsorship for his work from one of the firms present.

Nigel wondered if it would have been better had Judith accompanied him. But he was also aware that the presence of his wife might have made things even worse. An unused table setting had stared glumly at him throughout the first two courses before a waitress in fish-net tights had deigned to remove it, finally accepting his assurance that he was destined to remain un-partnered throughout this evening of forced merry-making. It was so difficult, Judith had certainly seemed keen to come and then, just as he was pulling on his brown suede jacket over the retro-1960's black polo-neck sweater, she lay flat out on the bed and put her hand over her eyes, "You go on your own, I'm staying here." There was not even time for a decent argument.

Upon the low platform that was serving as a temporary stage, imaginary drums rolled. All that was needed to complete the ghastly scenario was for the MC to announce a 'commercial break', but in the absence of such the sweaty little man extracted a card from its envelope with a flourish, emulating every flourish that he had flourished throughout the whole tedious evening.

"The winner is . . ." the imaginary drum roll stopped, ". . . Mr Nigel Marston with his sexy poem of love and romance – The Pale."

Nigel froze. Slowly he lowered the glass of sweet fizzy wine that had been approaching his lips, grim stuff it was, but elixir to one seeking an escape from total sobriety. This could not be happening to him. How could he have brought that particular, possibly charming but excruciatingly lightweight and hardly prize-winning poem to this awful place? Why had he been so stupid as to enter the competition? He had offered up a piece of himself, somewhat hackneyed it was true, but an intimate web of words and emotion. Now it had been ingested in totality by these all-consuming sharks of commercialism that were circling around him, circling closer and ever closer. There was no way out.

The whole ballroom turned towards him. Face after face; table after table of faces; serried ranks of faces – and each one of them was baring its teeth at him, mouths fixed in a rictus of false praise. He sensed rather than saw the green-eyed approximation of support emanating from those fellow poets who were seated with him. Behind their beaming congratulatory smiles metaphorical hands shifted, their fingers better able to tightly clasp around concealed literary daggers.

Real hands were now clapping, smashing one into another, creating a deafening, ever-shifting wall of sound that bounced off the ceiling and reverberated around the walls before wreaking destruction upon assembled eardrums. More hands were raising him from the faux-gold arms of his upholstered chair revealing its deep crimson padding, peppered as it was with whole armies of minuscule yellow stars.

Nigel stumbled his way to the raised dais where many decades ago the resident Big Band had elegantly played a number of Viennese Waltzes. Hands patted his back with such fierceness that in unison they shoved him staggeringly forward. The MC, as resplendent and as uncompromising as a tamer of lions, stood waiting, still sweating slightly, and beaming at him. A moist hand was extended from this oh so jolly little man. It pumped Nigel's right arm, then professionally rotated him to face the room.

"Stay," mouthed the MC as if commanding an errant gundog. He then turned to the besuited bodies seated at tables whose crisp white tablecloths obscured the cheap reality of their plywood tops in some sort of bemused metaphor of the whole evening.

"Ladies and Gentlemen, it is my great pleasure, no, my very great pleasure to welcome our Special Guest Writer to present the Caesar Charleston prize. So please give a big hand for . . ."

"Oh God," thought Nigel, "Not again."

" . . . none other than . . . .Miss Josephine Debray."

More thunder from the audience as from the side door of the stage emerged the gothic presence of JDB. She floated, rather than walked to the podium, her ample frame swathed in things black that boasted a trail of golden tendrils. This doyen passé of the literary scene held up a plump white hand to hush the expected adulation, but not so urgently that she could not indulge herself in it.

Nigel stared at the woman. He vaguely recalled some radio show that had, very briefly, discussed her work. As far as he could remember it had been met with thinly disguised contempt from whatever literary critics had been strutting their stuff on that exceedingly pretentious programme. He was not ashamed to admit that had never read anything written by this bountiful vision.

"I am so privileged that little me has been asked here this evening by no lesser personage than Lord Acton to present this important award that his Foundation has so generously donated as this year's Caesar Charleston prize."

The audience once again erupted, whilst a well-built rather florid man half rose from the nearest table thereby acknowledging his own presence. He made a tiny bow in the direction of JDB. His Lordship was a man of manufacture rather than culture, and no doubt due to his making a truly munificent donation to the Ruling Party, had been recently elevated to the peerage.

"I am all too well aware," cooed JDB, "of how our wonderful poets of today are struggling against the overwhelming tide of Modernism in an almost vain attempt to stem the copious outpouring of Free Verse, and this in the face of something of a drought in government funding."

His Lordship scowled slightly, and Josephine, sensing his discomfort added, "such being, of course, only the result of the most carefully targeted of initiatives towards industrial sponsorship." Acton relaxed.

Nigel stared out above the heads of the well-dined attendees. He did not look at the multi-faceted ceiling ball, nor did he focus upon the golden tassels of the crimson pelmets. His spirit picked him up and transported him to the open moorland above his grey stone house. He could hear the bleat of the new-born early lambs and smell the musky scent of the peat-bearing beck. High above him an Elgarian lark ascended, singing its own harmony in tribute to that great composer. Here, in this imagined English countryside, his spirit could rise and fall like that bird, untamed and untainted by the false splendour and fading promise of the Grand Hotel - and all who were currently sinking within her.

"... to that wonderful poet, Mr Nigel Marston."

A few hands clapped, realized they were in a very small minority, regretted their mistake, and retreated to their owner's laps.

Had she finished? Why was everything 'wonderful'? Was he supposed to do something?

The MC manoeuvred Nigel obsequiously to just right of stage centre. The prime location that had been picked out by the Roving Spot, was of course fully occupied by the redoubtable JDB. The MC passed an oversize chunk of cardboard to the poetess. She held it out graciously, one edge towards Nigel, who duly took hold of it. Cameras flashed.

"I have great pleasure in presenting you, Mr ... ahem ... Nigel darling, with this incredibly generous cheque from the Acton for Action Trust." She proffered her cheek. Nigel negotiated all the formidable fleshy obstacles in the way of the presented target and administered the statutory smack at air.

He peered curiously over the top of the cardboard of which they both held an end. 'Pay' it said, followed by a hastily scrawled 'Nigel Marston'. The next line jigged into his view, 'the sum of Two hundred and Fifty pounds Only'. Nigel particularly liked the 'only'.

The MC ushered the Debray off stage and relieved Nigel of the cardboard cheque, propping it against the lectern. "So as a final treat, Ladies and Gentlemen, I will ask Nigel, I do hope I may call you Nigel, to recite his poem, The Pale."

Sotto voce Nigel responded with just a tremor of hope in his voice, "I don't have it with me."

"Look at the Autocue," whispered the MC. Hope died.

With remorseless efficiency the first verse appeared on the screen. He started to read:

> *We have strolled the forbidden garden;*
> *My silent love and I;*
> *We have drunk of the midnight perfumes,*
> *And caught starlight from the sky.*

Nigel's throat constricted.

He knew that the poem was doggerel, the saccharine-laden rhyming couplets that would be so eagerly seized upon and torn asunder by the critics, but he was a trifle put out to realise that he had already lost half his audience, most of whom were busying themselves in the all-important task of refilling their glasses. Those few that were still looking in his direction wore the patient fixed smiles of attendees at a Sunday sermon, uncomprehending and massively bored.

> *We have crossed the mighty oceans;*
> *My storm-tossed love and I.*
> *We have ridden the foaming wave-crests,*
> *And sucked the seas bone dry.*

He was having trouble making himself heard over the increasing level of conversation and the clink of so many bottles upon a myriad of glasses.

> *We have scaled the largest mountains;*
> *My light-foot love and I.*
> *We have climbed the highest summits,*
> *And watched as clouds pass by.*

> *We have wandered the darkest woodlands;*
> *My dappled love and I.*

> *We have counted the trees of the forest,*
> *And howled the wild wolf's cry.*

The MC signalled frantically to the sound engineer to increase the volume issuing from the speakers. Nigel lowered his microphone. A screeching howl erupted as feedback filled the hall, bouncing off the peeling, yellowish paint on the upper parts of the walls and hurling itself back at the now boisterous audience.

The MC leapt at Nigel pushing up his hand that held the Mic.

"Keep it up." He said. At that very moment the screeching ceased and, save for those words, reeking with double entendre, the hall fell silent. The phrase resonated around the quietened ballroom.

A snigger ran around the audience as the overdressed and over-stressed exchanged meaningful winks. "Keep it up, ho, ho!" There was no way forward now. Nigel surveyed the gaudy ties and glinting necklaces displayed upon the necks of their corporate owners, who were exhibiting all the signs of at least partial inebriation. The sniggering metamorphosed into a rumble of barely suppressed laughter that ran from table to table.

The MC called for silence. "Gentlemen, Gentlemen, please give our award-winning poet your attention."

Nigel fought against an overwhelming desire to run, to put as much space as he could between himself and this God-awful place with its God-awful audience.

> *We have loved with the wildest passion;*
> *My wanton love and I.*
> *When you steal through my open widow*
> *And fondle my naked thigh.*

The attendees were in the mood now, and no mistake. An extremely tedious evening of receiving awards for their business prowess had emboldened the recipients to regard this so-called poet as the walk-on comedy turn arranged specifically for their amusement. Nigel ploughed on amongst the catcalls and ribaldry, the end was in sight:

> *But now, Light Love, it's over,*
> *It is time to bid goodbye*
> *For though Moonlight shines forever*
> *Mere Mortal Man must die.*

Nigel stood quietly and alone, bombarded by roars of laughter and raucous shouts of 'Keep it up, Nige'.

For Nigel it was the final straw. The ghastly decaying ballroom decked out in its glitzy gold and crimson frippery, the sweaty little oh-so-funny MC, the podgy gothic eminence that, having left the limelight, had plumped itself down next to Acton, that parvenu of a hapless peer. And now his tender offering to the gentle moon, the muse of poesy, had been utterly destroyed. How dare they do such a thing. Nigel clutched his microphone and moved menacingly to the front of the low staging.

"Fuck off," he said. "Fuck off the whole fucking lot of you."

The MC laid a restraining hand upon the arm holding the microphone.

"And particularly, Fuck Off You," said Nigel., turning the man around and gently propelling him towards the back of the stage.

The podium boasted an old-fashioned microphone cable upon which the MC tripped and in doing so hurled himself headlong into the backcloth, which collapsed around him revealing recently painted scenery, that of a tableaux depicting what appeared to be a Roman orgy.

It seemed to Nigel that this was curiously apposite.

The MC unrolled himself from the backcloth and decided that he must remove the poet. He sidled around the far side of the now deserted podium and placed himself squarely in front of Nigel, making a successful grab for the microphone. For one, short, moment it looked as though he might regain control of the situation, however the unfortunate man had been startled by the ease with which he had wrested the mic from Nigel's grip and, unbalancing, took a pace to his rear. With a howl of surprise and fear he tripped backwards off the staging falling heavily upon the floor. Unaware that the mic was still live he uttered the immortal words "Shit, my bum hurts!" The audience bayed with laughter and the photographer from the Gazette snapped a frame that the next day would be syndicated, to his great profit.

Nigel was feeling sick, he was exhausted, and above all he wanted out of here. He could no longer be associated in any further way with this tawdry award ceremony. In a final attempt to preserve his own dignity, and the dignity of poets the world over, he walked firmly and finally from the ballroom, leaving behind him a mixed scene of devastation and hilarity

With a feeling of the greatest relief he stood upon the front steps of The Grand Hotel and drew in a deep breath. Then, to the distress of three blue-rinsed ladies from the USA who had just alighted from their taxi, he threw back his head and bellowed to the world in general "Bloody, bloody, hell!"

(Lake **District, UK**)

Twenty miles of navigating a Land Rover through late evening traffic had a strangely calming effect. The uncompromising driving position coupled with the roughness of the ride served both to sooth

Nigel's wild thoughts and focus his mind on what he had achieved rather than leave him mulling morosely over the disaster of that awful prize-giving.

Two miles from home he pulled off the minor road at Mile Cross and switched off the vehicle's headlights. Down in the valley the half dozen sodium lights of the village stabbed their way into the surrounding darkness, whilst the almost full moon was draping the high fells beyond in a comforting veil of light. It was a view that he knew so well and that he could never tire of, by moonlight or in full sunshine.

His approach to the aesthetic of landscape was almost reverential. Here was not just the wonderful contrast between lush meadows, bosky forest trees, and the starkness of the high fells, but beneath the very obvious surface beauty there lay a wealth of meaning concealed within the rich resource of landscape and social history. It was ingrained in the very fabric of the countryside. The stone walls that ran so straight and uncompromising up the steep fell-sides intakes of Napoleonic enclosure, the deciduous woodland once so prized in Elizabethan times for the oak that had made England the sea-power that she then was, the Herdwick that had caused such petitions in Chancery because of their wanderings from one monastic sheepwalk to another in the days before they acquired the ability to hold a heaf.

Truth be told such thoughts were but a device for him to further delay his homecoming. Judith had been left lying on their large double bed. Outwardly, even in her mid-forties, she still retained much of her once stunning looks, but inwardly she was a changed and changing woman, far removed from the fun-loving vivacious girl that he had married. In those days they both had several drinks every evening, and he thought nothing of it. As time went on he became aware that Judith was drinking a little more than he was but, he reasoned, that was because he had to keep a clear head for those early morning starts of his.

Judith had been quick-witted although never particularly acute of intellect. Her boundless energy and her ability to charm everybody that she met had been an inspiration to him. Even in the early days of their marriage she had her quieter weeks, but he accepted those as a more reflective part of her nature, not realising that such mood swings were occasioned by her drinking.

The problem had however become more pronounced, especially after Caroline, their second and last child, had gone to secondary school. Perhaps the physical involvement in caring for her young children had helped her stave it off, but by the time she reached her late thirties she was an alcoholic, and a very difficult and unpredictable one. Perhaps there was more than an element of what was originally called manic depression and was now referred to as bi-polar disease, but there was no getting away from the root cause.

Nigel worried about their future. He had been successful in selling the boat chandlery and had done pretty well out of that sale. He was happy about that although both he and Judith had worked hard for many years to build things up to the stage where the business could be sold well as a going concern. They had both been in their late twenties and it had not been easy setting up a boat chandlery, especially with two very young children. The large outfits around Windermere had leaned on them in an unfriendly way for some years, but with his knowledge of boats, and Judith's eye for stylish clothing they had survived, and more than survived, they had done well. How different Judith had been then. If he was struggling with a contract she had used her charm and motivational skills to snatch success out of potential disaster.

It was getting cold sitting in the Land Rover with its rudimentary heater. Even with the almost spring-like days the nights could be decidedly chilly. Winter had not finally released its grasp. With some reluctance he started the engine.

"Hi, Judith, I'm back."

He was hardly expecting a response. He walked through to the den, pulled the Poetry Award invitation card from his pocket and dropped it into the bin. He looked at it nestling there between a rotting apple core and the discarded draft of a poem that he had been working on and smiled, it seemed an appropriate resting point, half way between creation and disintegration. In an absent-minded way he gathered the random scattering of books that adorned his desk with the intention of returning them to their allotted places on his shelves, however there was a cry from the Sitting Room, "Is that you, Nige?"

The summons was imperative, so leaving the books on the corner of his desk he went in search of his wife, finding her ensconced in her favourite comfortable chair, a bottle by her side. The television was on, but he doubted if she was, or had been, watching it. Neither of them liked football. He switched it off and turned towards her.

"Hello, dearest, how are you feeling now?"

His wife turned towards him, her face a picture of sadness and rejection. The Siamese raised itself from her lap yawned, stretched, and lazily eased its body onto the floor. Judith pushed a few wisps of hair from in front of her blue eyes and focused her gaze upon her husband.

"How could you leave me?" It was clear that she was angry, but she was also close to tears, "I've been here all alone for ages and ages. Where on earth have you been?"

"You know very well. I was at that poetry award ceremony that we were going to together."

"Was I? I don't remember. Poetry, that's nice."

"You decided not to come.

"I couldn't. I just couldn't," a single tear started to trickle down her face. "I don't know what's wrong with me. It doesn't make sense."

Nigel felt a sudden compulsion to protect this unhappy woman. It was not by positive choice that she had come to this. "It doesn't matter," he said.

"I would have come with you, was it fun?"

"No, it wasn't," said Nigel as memories of the Grand Hotel started to flood into his mind, "It was bloody awful. But I won that prize, you know."

"But all the same, I should have come."

"You know what, I actually won that bloody prize."

"I would have been there with you. It would have been . . ." she seemed to search for a bigger word," . . . nice."

"Pretty measly really, only £250 and they haven't even given it to me yet."

Judith was fiddling with the sleeve of her dress. She seemed to be trying to get it underneath her watchstrap and becoming more and more enraged that she could not do so. Nigel looked at her, wondering. Sometimes she would still be able to hold a serious and, if not intellectually rigorous, at least cogent conversation. Then there were times like this when she seemed to drift off into her own world. He considered rather vaguely how contented she might be. They had both been very happy once, indeed for the first half of their twenty-something years together. Now happiness seemed to elude her, indeed he was uncertain as to whether she continued to seek for it.

He had tried to fill his life, his creative impulses, with poetry. A couple of years ago he had attended a creative writing course in Kendal. He had enjoyed it, not so much for the content but more for the interaction with people. He had not realized that he was lonely but he enjoyed the companionship of being caught up, albeit briefly, in the lives of others. He still kept in touch with some of them. They met once a month and read their latest poetic efforts to each other, but again he stayed with the group more for the pleasing company that such meetings offered rather than the versifying output that issued therefrom.

He turned again to his wife. "Have you had any supper?"

She shrugged, indicating that either she had, or she had not, but either way she did not much care.

The phone rang. It was Caroline, phoning from London. "Hi, Nige." From their earliest days he had encouraged both her and Jimmy to call him by his Christian name and the shortened version seemed to have just emerged from that. This first name thing from his children had seemed a little odd, a little 'ultra-lefty' at first, but now that they were adults it put them all at an equal standing, and he liked that. "How did it go?"

"I won the bloody thing, Caro, but you wouldn't believe how awful the ceremony was. You know the Grand, well it's become a really grotty place and it was full of the most ghastly business people tonight."

"Well done indeed. Was that the moonlight one that I laughed at so much?"

"Just so, but those heathens thought it was about a randy old lover."

Nigel could hear the delight in his daughter's voice. She had supported him wholeheartedly in the renaissance of his poetry.

"Did Mum enjoy it?" Judith had taken a different view about how children should address their parents.

"I'm afraid she didn't make it. Had a bit of a do."

"Oh, no. Is she OK now? I know she is in a bad way, but honestly, Nige, it's you who's bearing the brunt of it. You need to be careful; you must pace yourself."

"I'm fine, darling, and Judith is pretty good right now."

"And you won – that's brilliant. Did they give you loads of dosh?"

"Two hundred and fifty pounds"

"Bloody hell, that won't do much to keep the wolf from the door – oh well don't spend it all at once."

"Do you want to have a quick word with your mother?"

Nigel knew that Judith would find it hard to speak to Caroline, but Caro was good at keeping in touch and would do her best to cheer her up.

"It's Caro," said Nigel, "she wants a word."

"Of course it is, you idiot. Here let me speak to her." With a surprising degree of strength Judith wrenched the phone from his hand and walked, a trifle over exuberantly, towards the kitchen.

Nigel returned to the den and sat down at his desk. It was the bleakness of it all, he thought. He could manage his wife with the help of Zenca, the Polish woman who lived in the village. He thought he would be able to do so for some time, but he missed any form of meaningful communication. Judith had been very amusing company in her day and had been good fun to have around, enjoying a bit of joshing and verbal banter with him and their friends. He missed the sex as well. He was perplexed as to why she had rejected his every attempt to make love to her for the past year. Things had not been that good for some time before then, but they had sex once or twice every week when they were both in the mood.

He hit the space bar and his computer screen came alive. Slightly furtively he navigated to the Caesar Charleston page. 'Vanity,' he thought, 'All is Vanity.' His name was there, highlighted against 'Romantic Poet of The Year', and one click took him to The Pale. There was nothing there yet about the ruckus at The Grand, nor was there any sort of Bio about him, for both these exclusions he was profoundly grateful, although he noted that his e-mail address had been posted as a hyperlink, presumably so that potential publishers could beat a path to his door. He smiled gently at the ridiculous thought.

He could hardly have foreseen the success of this venture of his into a poetry competition. Since his mid-teens he had enjoyed scribbling the odd bit of verse.

In the early days, at boarding school, he and some of his friends had tried to set poetry to jazz – in the style of Christopher Logue of Red Bird fame. This had not been that successful; he wanted their syncopation to match his stanzas, whilst his three musician friends felt that they had first call and he should fit his verse to their music.

The door moved just enough to allow passage for the Siamese, white with dark brown points. Nigel was not a lover, or even a liker, of cats, however he had agreed to their having this feline as a pet, a Siamese being the nearest thing in the cat world to a dog. It leaped effortlessly, despite its 15 years, onto his desk and stalked around to his side, her tail erect.

"Go on, Tids, bugger off you nosey feline, and get your paws off my keyboard."

He turned the animal around so it would walk away from him. Seeking solace it pushed its back against the book pile and rubbed hard against it. The books tottered and fell with a resounding crash. The cat made a wild leap for safety, legs outstretched and claws deployed. She hit the curtains about a metre above the floor and dropping to the ground accompanied by the sound of rending material, she fled the room.

Far from being upset Nigel was grinning to himself as he picked the books up one by one, replacing them in the larger of the two bookshelves with care, distracted only by the notion of thousands of words clattering to the floor. Was it a cat-aided bid for literary freedom, or merely a symptom of rejection?

He pulled out the lower left-hand drawer of the desk and looked in a somewhat disinterested fashion at a cut-glass tumbler and a bottle of Johnny Walker. He changed his mind and closed the drawer.

| 38 |

3 |

(Athens, Greece)

Immediately after that first night when Anna experienced the expiation of her grief and her anger, she set about dealing with the formalities associated with a death.

She called Petros in the USA. Without making a fuss, she told him of his brother's death in a car accident, telling him that Panos had been returning home from a professional trip. "I'll make all the arrangements for the funeral," she told him, "Most likely it will be early next week."

"Not sure if we can get there that quickly."

"Well, I suppose we could delay it a couple of days until you and Dora can get a flight to Greece." She said nothing about Panos having a second wife and two children. She dealt in a similar fashion with all the people that needed to be informed and invited, friends and colleagues, his aunts and uncles. The list was not very long and due to the way that she now knew Panos had been betraying her she found it easy to distance herself from the reality of losing her husband.

She wondered why Panos had never suggested divorcing her. If he was happy with that Stella then why did he spend weekends in Athens pretending that he was happily married to his wife? There were no clues as to his thinking but Anna suspected that he rather enjoyed the challenge of outwitting her. If so then it amplified further her recognition of the cruel side of his nature.

She left her parents until last. To them she just added the small white lie that it had been Panos' wish - intimated in earlier discussions between them - that he should not be buried when he died, but rather that he should be cremated. "I really feel I must do exactly what he wished regarding this, although we will have to send his body to be cremated in Bulgaria."

Her parents lived in Chalkis, the provincial town near the village that her father had originally come from, and they had no contact with Panagiotis' world. They were terribly upset of course, worried about her and wondering why she had not told them about it as soon as it had happened. She made a laborious effort to dissuade her mother from getting on the next bus to Athens. "Don't worry, Mum, I promise I will come and see you as soon as I feel a little better." It seemed to work.

She was astonished at how well she was able to manage. She organized things and performed all the different parts of a procedure that had initially seemed insurmountable.

Then she went to see Ellie. It was queerly amusing to watch Ellie's eyes widen in total astonishment as she impassively recounted the details of her situation. She left Ellie no room for emotion, for she knew she would break down if she saw pity in Ellie's eyes or if she heard a single word of sympathy from her. All she wanted was to ask a single question that burnt shamefully within her. What rights did this Stella have to Panos's money and their belongings?

After fourteen years of marriage, they had little enough in the way of savings. They had acquired two cars, one now almost completely destroyed, and they still owed money on the mortgage of their beautifully furnished apartment. She made it clear to Ellie that the country cottage was her property, and that she had paid all the outgoings for it over the years of her marriage.

Her painting had developed from her taking a degree in Fine Arts, and she had been successful in selling a few pieces now and then, putting nearly all the proceeds into the cottage. The rest of their money, mainly Panos' income, had been used to pay the instalments on the apartment, to cover the cost of running the cars, and to meet all the other household expenses. Most of the little that she had managed to save she spent on Panos' funeral. She would be lucky if she could survive on what she had.

Ellie was quick to catch both her friend's mood and her unspoken question. They had known each other for such a long time and a large degree of mental empathy existed between them. Ellie was therefor well aware of what it was that Anna was so wishing to know, but ashamed to ask about.

"I'm sure that you don't have to worry about your house in the country. It was yours before you were married, and that was long before there was any question of this second family, which, of course," she continued without waiting for a response from Anna, "brings us to the only thing that they could have a claim on, his pension".

Anna waited in silence.

Ellie sighed. "Anna, I have never come across a case quite like this before, so don't take this as my final professional opinion, I'll look into it and come back with accurate information, but it seems to me the existence of children with this partner of his is likely to complicate things. Do you know anything about the woman? Does she work? Does she have any property?"

Anna did not have the slightest idea other than Stella having told her that she and Panos owned the house in Thessaloniki.

"If she doesn't have substantial assets, enough to sustain her two children, she'll probably take you to court Anna," Ellie looked worried. She was concerned about the position that her friend had found herself in. Anna shrugged; she really did not want to know about anything that concerned this second family.

On the day of the funeral, and just a couple of hours before Panos' mother and brother landed at Athens airport, Anna gathered a couple of suitcases. Into these she packed a basic amount of clothing, a dozen of her favourite poetry books, and her laptop. She locked the apartment and loaded the suitcases and the very few belongings that she had decided that she needed into her car. Amongst these there was no canvas, no oil-paints, no brushes, no turps. Following the night that she had spent on the floor of her studio she had closed its door so as to isolate it from the rest of the house. She could not bear even the slightest smell of oil-paint. She could not tolerate the sight of a canvas or easel or brush. She had left behind these painful reminders as tokens of a life she did not recognize, one that she did not wish to be associated with anymore. Quite why it was her painting that provoked such a negative response was unclear to her. She just knew that she had to abandon that part of her life, to disown it, to expunge it from her system.

Ellie would take care of the sale of the apartment and it seemed as if the money from that would be adequate to pay off the mortgage. She told Ellie that if it became clear that Stella's children were going to claim rights over Panos' pension then she would not pursue the matter. Going to court over such issue, even if she were to win the case, would take from her much more than the money was worth. After all, they were Panos' children, although sadly not hers, and might really need the money. This was not altruism; it was a defense mechanism against any form of involvement in her late husband's other life.

Ellie went mad with her. "Are you out of your mind woman?" she cried out in disbelief. "Haven't you realized what's going on around you? This country has not yet recovered from the financial crisis. News from the international press is discouraging and from that quarter there is still an almost hysterical condemnation of our country. In every political or economic analysis that I've read or heard lately, there's always the same message, 'Things will not get better for a long time'. What are you going to live on? For Christ's sake, Anna, this pension is your only financially solid ground, and after all those years of marriage you're certainly entitled to a major portion of it!" Ellie had been gasping with despair, trying with increasing desperation to get her friend to see the precariousness of her position. But Anna had not changed her mind.

(Evia, Greece, 7 weeks later)

Thick dollops of rain fell upon the glass of the large balcony door, resounding with a frequent, successive plop, plop, plop, and forming innumerable little blobs on the glass before growing large enough to overflow, and roll on downwards. The smaller streams would combine with other larger ones that would eventually meet the end of their journey at the bottom edge of the pane.

Anna stood by the door, observing the rivulets, and remembering how A. A. Milne had written a poem about two raindrops on a window pane. She looked away at the misty fields with their olive and citrus trees that spread around her, half-encircled by a series of mountains, now faintly discernible through the downpour. The sea was a wide grey smudge in the distance, inseparably merging into the greyness of the sky in a way that made it really hard to tell where the one ended and the other began. It was mid-March, and the year was moving towards the end a winter that had not offered anything by way of substantial snowfall but which had soaked the fields with massive amounts of rain.

This cottage was truly hers, and had been since before she married Panos. It had been left to her in the will of her paternal grandmother, her beloved Γιαγιά, who had seen within her young granddaughter the makings of a half-decent artist. "Annoula," she had said, using the Greek diminutive, "this cottage of mine will be yours, after my time. It is a very special place and I want you to feel its peace. If ever you are troubled or in crisis, bring yourself here. It will not heal you, but here you will be able to heal yourself." In so saying she had shown great prescience.

Her grandmother had died just after Anna's twenty-first birthday and she had come here then to mourn the passing of that gentle soul. Now it she was here, in need of calming, and to find her way in life once more. There was surely no better place than this small cottage, situated just above the surrounding olive groves, and within sight of the sea. She hadn't changed much, just renewed some of the windows and a couple of doors, being careful to do so in the local idiom. There was running water, electricity, and a rather basic sewerage system. Since the cottage had become hers she had re-painted the outside walls with limewash every three years and painted the window frames and other woodwork that intense blue of the islands. There was only one, rather small, bedroom, and a slightly larger kitchen. The living room was a decent size for a cottage and boasted a large open fireplace with an ornate metal log grate.

And now, here she was, living in such a different manner after her life had taken such a dramatic change; happy in this country cottage away from people, loud voices, half-truths, and lies. She did not have a television; and she did she want one. She had always found it so sad that people that lived on their own would spend their days sitting in front of a television set, watching rubbish. For many people it is human interaction, relationships, gossip that bring meaning to their lives, and the soaps on the TV provided just this. It was a way for the lonely to occupy their minds. After a few weeks she realized she could do with a radio, for she had to keep in some sort of touch with the rest of the world. She found radio more versatile, less offensive, and its output more colourful.

Ellie would visit from time to time. For the first couple of months she would, every week, drive the one hundred kilometers or so that separated them, but as time went on Anna begged her not to come so often as it was the best part of a four hour round trip and Ellie would be spending a fortune on petrol. So these visits became less frequent although the two of them kept in regular touch by phone.

Her parents had also come to see her. They had stayed for a whole week. She had given them her bedroom whilst she slept on the sofa in the living room. It had not been an easy week, having to conjure up excuses and come up with all sorts of lies to keep Panos' double life from her parents had been mentally exhausting for her. Although the cottage had belonged to his mother Ellie's father, Georgos, had never lived there. His childhood home had been in Chalkis where he and his wife, Katerina, still lived. He had been fit and strong as a young man, working on the railway. However, he had developed a disease that affected his heart valves, endocarditis they had called it and although it had been caught early enough to treat with antibiotics it had still left him weak, and his heart very vulnerable.

Katerina was some six years younger than her husband and originated from Athens, where her parents had lived after escaping the destruction of Smyrni by the Turks in 1922. Anna never knew how her parents had met and was just slightly too embarrassed to ask.

She moved away from the balcony door and turned to add one more log to the fire. Dusk was fast approaching, bringing the temperature on what had been a particularly cold day to an even lower level. She disliked being cold. When Ellie, on one of her last visits, had seen how she liked to overload the fire, she had remonstrated with her hinting at the uncertain finances of both Anna and the whole country. Anna had laughed in a careless way, exhibiting a mood that she did not really feel, "I'd rather go hungry than feel cold".

Despite her bravado Anna feared that with the prices of basic goods rising at a speed nobody could keep up with, her position might become really serious. It did not seem that things were going to improve, but she had to stay positive, after all she had half of Panos' pension and her lifestyle now was not at all financially demanding. To be fair to her that Stella person had not been particularly greedy. She had only asked for half of Panos's pension, as security for the children, particularly as she was not sure how long she would be able to keep her job after the massive wave of lay-offs in their city. Anna knew this was probably true. Stella had added, in a conciliatory manner and without a trace of threat that she didn't wish to take the case to court. Perhaps she just did not want to risk an unfavorable verdict. It did not make much difference to Anna, she just did not want to think about such matters.

Perhaps she should be grieving. Indeed she felt as if she was grieving, but for what. She could hardly be doing so for that duplicitous philanderer who had torn apart all that she had held dear in her marriage. Perhaps it was the marriage itself, but certainly of late that had not been something to look back upon with pleasure. With startling insight she realized that this grief of hers was self-pity. A longing for that which she had been, and could be no more. The loss of an innocent part of her soul. A roadblock to her artistic creativity. Yet she had found a way to circumvent this.

She sat at her desk, a wooden kitchen table she used for the purpose as a matter of convenience. She preferred eating at the large coffee table in front of the sofa. The truth being that she, like many other lonely people on this earth, had a strong aversion to eating alone at her dining table. On her desk she had placed her laptop computer, all her poetry books, and a few drafts of her own attempts at poetry, these being, in her opinion, rather disappointing. Poetry had become her new refuge, both as the nurturer of her troubled soul and as an outlet for her creativity. She just wished she were as good at poetry as she had been in painting.

She switched on her computer and clicked on the website she had marked for return. "On the Verge of Poetry" was an English site for either amateur or unpublished poets. She liked that name. She found the gentle humour in it matched her own feelings. Current Greek poetry was so full of sadness and loss and such poetry sites as she had visited had, it seemed, fallen victims to an entropy that left them lifeless. As she was fluent in English, thanks to an excellent teacher and her parents paying for lessons at the local Frontisteria, it seemed natural for her to search for English poetry sites.

"On the Verge of Poetry" was well organized, amusing, and offered her a world untouched by the troubles that had beset southern Europe. There she found all sorts of news regarding poetry, latest publications as well as classic, well-known works and a very large collection of beautiful poems that the registered members of the site had posted there. At times she was tempted, perhaps she should post a couple of her own too? Despite her competency in the language she felt inadequate and had never found the courage to do so. She thought that her efforts just would not stand up to the level and the skill of the poems she had seen there. Of course there were also mediocre, amateur poems like hers, but she did not believe in the vanity of presenting one's work unless it really deserved to be read. She had thus remained merely as a reader.

On the home page of the site there was a news piece, with the indication "HOT" flashing next to the headline "Nigel awarded! A chronicle of a disaster." Curious, she clicked on it. She read "Nigel Marston, one of our site's most long-term members, was yesterday awarded the annual prize of the Caesar Charleston Foundation for his poem 'The Pale'. However, the award ceremony, held in the Grand Hotel's central ballroom, was turned into a farce." It went on to describe the evening and Nigel's eventual withdrawal from the ceremony.

She remembered "The Pale". It had not been a particularly good poem in the technical sense, but it had moved her, not for any pretense to lyrical verse nor for any skill that Nigel might have shown in portraying something inanimate, the moon, with such passion. What she had enjoyed was the wit, the humour, the gentle misleading of the reader to believe he was describing an affair between two people. She too had always been a moon-lover and yet she thought she would never have succeeded in giving it so much life.

Poor Nigel, she totally empathized; she knew what the distinction of an award would mean to an unpublished poet, the hope and expectation that would raise. She could then also imagine his disappointment, the shame. She normally avoided direct communication with members of the site. She might on occasion leave a comment or cast her vote for poems she liked the most, but that was about all she was prepared to do. She was sure she would embarrass herself if she posted either of her English poems, or communicated with any of the authors.

But in that incident Nigel had been on the losing side, and she considered that unfair. She clicked on the link that brought up his email address. After a few minutes of thought, she wrote:

Dear Nigel,

You don't know me. My name is Anna, I am Greek and until recently lived in Athens. I have been a reader on the site for the past few months. I have looked at most of the poems you have uploaded and have really enjoyed them, "The Pale" being among the ones that amused me the most, and which I most empathized with. So I just felt impelled to write and congratulate you upon winning a prize for this delightful, witty, poem.

Sincerely,

Anna

She sent the message and switched off her computer, slightly puzzled by her own brashness in writing.

She needed to get an early night as she had to wake up almost at dawn the next morning. The earlier she arrived at the Prefecture Office the more chances she would have of getting a decent place in the queue. Queues in such offices tended to be almost endless, hardly allowing any progress towards the desk where she would ask of the official whether there was any news about her application for the surrogate post of fine arts teacher at the local high-school.

(Lake District, UK.)

The morning dawned bleak and cold. Nigel's had suffered a restless night cringing at his own behaviour in walking out, when he was being honoured as a poet – how often would such chances come his way again?

Breakfast had done little to dispel his black mood. Even Judith had noticed it, which was most unusual for her. "Bit grumpy today aren't we," she had said in the manner of a specialist doing her rounds at the local hospital.

"Bloody ceremony, yesterday."

But his wife's attention was already elsewhere, her mind skipping away on a journey of its own.

Zenca had arrived and was flourishing the paper. "You are famous, Mr Marston, you are in the local news."

Nigel reached out to take the newspaper from the girl, but Judith was quicker than him and grabbed it. Zenca had already folded the paper to one of the middle pages, and she was pointing to something that was making Judith smile, a rarity in itself. Nigel got up from his chair and walked with considerable foreboding made his way around the table so that he was standing behind his wife.

"Well, dear, now that you are a well-known, if not an established, poet I am sure you will win many more prizes, possibly for the martial arts rather than the poetic ones." Her own humour set Judith giggling, much to his annoyance.

"Not if I can bloody help it," he said. He gathered up his coffee cup and walked rather stiffly out of the room, his wife still chortling to herself and rather more than a trace of a smile playing upon Zenca's lips.

Nigel sat himself resolutely at his desk. He was finished as a poet. Never again would colleagues, or the public, take him seriously. The fact that he had never lashed out at that obnoxious little man was irrelevant, the photo said it all, and if it had made The Guardian it would no doubt already be in most of the other Nationals. Perhaps it would be possible to just to curl up and die, here in his den.

The phone rang. "Is that Nigel Marston?"

"I am he."

"Mr Marston, Nigel if I may, I wonder if you could tell me a little about your adventures last night?"

"I don't remember much about it. To whom am I speaking?"

"I was just wondering if you regret not collecting that prize?"

"Not at all, I don't give a damn about money, who are you?"

"You might like to know that Mr Bloxham, the Master of Ceremonies that you had a bit of a struggle with, only sustained a few bruises."

"Pity. If you do not tell me who you are I shall put the phone down on you."

'Thank you so much, Nigel, we really appreciate your frankness."

"What do you mean? I haven't said a thing."

"Oh but you have, you have been most helpful. I'm just reading back from my notes: 'Nigel, an award-winning poet with an unenviable reputation for violence, told our reporter that he did not give a damn about the Caesar Charleston Award. He had attended the lavish ceremony at which wine flowed freely and admitted to our man that he did not remember much about the event, but that money meant very little to him anyway. When asked about his concern for the Master of Ceremonies who had been injured after a struggle with him, Nigel said that it was a pity the man had not suffered even greater injuries than those that he had inflicted.' See what I mean Nigel? The Journal is most grateful to you for the interview."

Nigel lowered the phone from his ear and touched the red button. Then, very deliberately, he pushed the green button. He was not taking any further calls this morning. He felt anger, more with himself than with anyone else and, truth be told, he was wallowing in self-pity.

The Mac Mail application on his desktop pinged. He turned towards the machine dreading what was to come. Any message to him this morning could only be about one thing. He clicked on the icon.

His Mac Mail mailbox was showing an incoming message. He wondered why people bothered to gloat over his misfortune. It seemed to be from someone calling herself Anna. No doubt some sycophantic well-wisher from the Poetry website who would be offering heartfelt sympathies. Nigel bristled at the thought.

As he read the e-mail his self-pity and anger began to evaporate. He reached for the mouse and hovered the cursor over the 'Return' button. He thought better of it, what was the point? He had enough troubles to contend with already without corresponding with some foreign woman, however empathetic she might appear. With a deep sigh he rose from his chair and walked through to the dining room. Judith was still sitting at the table. She seemed to be lost in thought.

"Just going out for a bit of a wander. Want to clear my head. See you later."

His wife barely acknowledged him. Her slightly hysterical laughing moment was now a thing of uncertain memory. She inclined her head just a fraction, then returned to whatever wild ideas were coursing through her head.

The moorland track stretched out ahead of Nigel, inviting, not demanding, that his boots should tramp it. The sun was already gaining height in a cloudless sky of the palest blue and the way ahead was firm and inviting. Regretting only the absence of a canine companion, Nigel viewed the prospect of an hour's gentle exercise with both anticipation and relief.

'Tramping it out', is how he saw the joy that a walk such as this would bring him. The rhythmic stomp of his boots on the firm trackway and the swaying of his body to the tune of the countryside, there really was no better therapy.

Despite the glorious moorland scenery, with the weak sunshine trying its best to pull the budding leaves out of the overwintered larch, Nigel found it hard not to allow his mind to wander back to the problem that beset Judith, and of course the impact that was having on both their lives. For the first dozen or more years of their marriage Judith would have been walking along beside him, keeping him company, chattering, laughing and chasing after the children. A family that was as happy as any other. But unbeknownst to both of them dark clouds had been looming.

And now both the children had upped and deserted the nest, both Jimmy and Caroline lived in London, busy pursuing flourishing careers, both with partners and, for Caroline at least, the prospect of marriage this year. Already he had dropped a hint to his intelligent daughter that a wedding in London might be the easiest option. She had hardly batted an eyelid at the suggestion; she knew the score and did not want to put her mother under any more stress.

And what would Judith be doing now, he thought. Perhaps still sitting in the Dining Room, or had she wandered through to the conservatory, staring out into the garden through unseeing eyes.

There had been little response, hardly a flicker when he left. The same thing had happened the other day when he told her he was off to the shops, she had not responded at all then. He had gone up to her and taken her by the shoulders, intending to turn her to face him. Judith had started to her feet, half tripping backwards, an expression of terror on her face.

"It's OK, OK," he said, reaching for and holding her left hand. She grabbed it away from him and cringing back as she did so, her hair falling as a shielding mantle around her shoulders. It was appalling, for several moments she had not recognised him and had, he realized, been terrified that he would do her harm.

Ahead of him now the track came to a decision-demanding fork. He marched firmly to the right although he had no idea why. Impulses were important to him now. For so much of his life he had been a decision-maker where logic and the weighing of the pros and cons were a vital ingredient of the business. Now he could afford to indulge in whimsy, to allow his left-brain to take over and to, as Jimmy would have put it, 'go with the flow'.

The path he was on turned out to be good. Like so many decisions that he had made in his life he could not say that it was better than the alternative might have been. Sufficient it was that the resulting way had turned out so well. He came to the edge of the moor. Beyond and below him lay the in-bye land, and a small lake.

He pushed on towards the fell gate where a flock of sheep were idling, no doubt awaiting fodder. The Swaledales parted to let him through. Two of the ewes, alive to the potential danger from this single human source, stamped their front feet to call to them their new-born lambs. One to each ewe they rushed at their mother's teats barging and suckling – their reward for heeding the call to avoid danger. Nigel craved their simple reaction. Uncertain happenings; signal to come to a safe haven; there to be nurtured. If only life, human life, his life, were that straightforward.

As he made his way homeward his thoughts turned to that woman, what was her name, that Greek person who had been kind enough to write to him? He wondered vaguely what inspired someone like that to bother to write about such a stupid little event that had taken place in a far-off country. It had been good though. He had enjoyed his increasing involvement in that poetry forum. He had found a few things there that had really inspired him, and some people who were able to provide mutual critique in a way that was so helpful to him. He had posted several of his works on the site and whilst he was a much more traditional poet than most of those active on the forum these offerings of his had been well received.

With a quickening pace he strode out for home. If this Greek woman could be bothered to write to him the least he could do was to return her e-mail.

Dear Anna,

I am so pleased that you enjoyed my poem 'The Pale'. It is a strange piece because although it reads like a love poem between two human lovers it is, as you will know, a romantic poem written to that most wonderful, but inanimate lover, the Moon. As a poet I am rather embarrassed by the crassness of my technique, but it was something that was determined to come out of me!

I fear that things did not go too well that evening and it rather marred my very first experience of receiving a prize for my efforts.

Do you write poetry? I have had it in me for most of my life, but only now have I found the time, and I suppose the inclination, to immerse myself in it.

Your written English is excellent – my Greek non-existent. Thank you so much for your support, I was having a fairly brutal day of it and I rather think that I would still be wallowing in self-pity but for your kind thoughts.

Best wishes
Nigel

He paused for nearly half a minute with the cursor over the 'Send' button. This person, Anna, had been kind in writing to him and he did want to thank her for that, however he really did not like the idea of any further discussion about the 'Affair at The Grand'. She seemed, from what she had said, to be aware of that, and although he had a suspicious mind he was fairly certain that she was genuine, not another journalist after a variation of the sordid little story.

He clicked the mouse.

4

<u>**(Evia, Greece)**</u>

The sign in the hallway at the Prefecture Office read 'Applications, Pending Applications, and Other Matters'. So it was that Anna stood patiently in the queue for the desk that was responsible for handling her submission for the post of surrogate art teacher.

The office opened its doors at seven o'clock in the morning, but by that time she found there were already some thirty or even forty people waiting ahead of her. She loathed this queuing, it was both diminishing and ridiculously time-consuming, but perhaps worse this standing still could make her spine go mad with rage. But public services seemed to thrive upon queuing. Even private enterprises were not exempt; she well remembered long queues at banks. She could hardly have expected things to improve at places such as this as unemployment was still at near record levels. Well, at least there were no more queues now at banks. Capital controls had seen to that.

She shifted her posture frequently, moving the weight of her body first to the right, then to the left, trying to comfort her back that was being tortured by pangs of the most excruciating pain. She had learned to live with this back problem that had plagued her since she had been involved in a motor bike accident in her late teens. She had been told that she had Sacroiliitis and whilst little could be done to cure the problem, the symptoms could be relieved by taking medication. Of course such treatment was expensive, even with her Greek health pass, her AMKA.

The woman in front of her had a compulsively irritating habit of frequently tossing back her long hair, perhaps as a unique way of marking more space in the queue. Anna stepped back to avoid yet another slap in face, but then she felt herself press into the belly of the man standing right behind her, as close to her waist as anybody had been for some time. She turned to look at him, half-embarrassed, half-reprimanding, and the man smiled awkwardly and took a pace back. But as he did so he stepped onto the foot of the woman standing behind him, who was now shouting at him, reproaching him for his carelessness.

Anna struggled to conceal a frown as she approached the desk. She was sure she had grown substantially older during the time she had been waiting, but she had every intention of being polite. After all, these people behind the desk had their own problems to deal with. They had to contend with innumerable customers, one after another, each with their own needs and problems. She tried a smile.

"Good-morning" she said in a manner as pleasing as she could manage with whilst trying not to cross the borders of formality.

The woman behind the desk looked at her gravely, with nothing but an expression of impatient inquisition in her eyes, and did not say a word. Anna placed the piece of paper with her application's registration number on the desk.

"I have come to ask whether there has been any news on my application?"

The woman peered at the piece of paper and looked at Anna suspiciously. "When did you apply?"

"Oh, on the 4th of October, the date is registered there, right under my application number I think."

"Wait a minute." The woman, without looking at her, disappeared behind what appeared to be a great filing rack for documents. There was a long wait. Eventually she came back with a large envelope in her hands.

"This is for you," she said. "The service was intending to mail it to you very shortly, but you came before we could do so."

It was almost a reprimand for taking up her valuable time. The envelope was thrust at her through the narrow space between the desk and a dirty Plexiglas board. Before Anna had even got it in her hands the woman had directed her attention to the next person and Anna understood that she had no option but to move on. She wanted to say 'thanks', but under the circumstances it was rather pointless.

The envelope remained unopened until Anna returned to her house. She could very well have opened it in the car before she drove home, but this envelope held her future, her chances to sustain herself financially and also psychologically, and she needed to open it in suitable and private surroundings.

Communication had become forbiddingly expensive of late so apart from Ellie's rare visits, or the short chats they had on their mobiles - they could not speak for long – and other than the occasional phone conversation with her parents she had not had any serious interaction with people for a considerable time. The polite "Good-morning" and "How are you?" that she would normally exchange with the shop-owners in the village did not count. Such niceties were always the same in that she made certain that she was civil, but also ensured that she kept a polite distance from these people. She could foresee, with dread, the questions and prying that would follow if she allowed herself to become involved in a real conversation, and that was the last thing that she wanted. Her personal life, and most particularly her past, was her own.

She sat herself down on the sofa. This was an important moment. Carefully she inserted a pencil under the flap of the envelope, and sliced it open. There was a single sheet of paper inside, which she reached for trembling slightly. There was just a brief paragraph saying that following her application for the post of surrogate teacher of fine arts at the province's high-school, she was granted the position and she should present herself to assume responsibility at the high-school, on the 1st of March. It was already February 16 and Anna wondered when they had been intending to mail this to her. It would have been very short notice if she had not collected it herself. But she was thrilled with the news.

Along with a barrage of new financial measures the government had cut down pensions to such an extent that they could not be considered substantial so much as disgraceful. Her pension from Panos was cut in half again. On top of that, she would have to pay what she considered to be an irrationally high tax for this small cottage she owned.

Ellie had said, "People who are still paying off the mortgage on their houses also pay this same tax."

"What will happen to people who are not able to pay?"

Ellie shrugged her shoulders, "I suppose they will have to leave."

"What are they expected to do after that?" said Anna, "Live in caves perhaps?"

She had never worked with children before, and was really looking forward to it. Perhaps it was a very small substitute for her not having had children of her own. How could that blasted husband of hers have lied to her in the way that he did? He had denied her birthright as a woman whilst at the same time fathering two children by that Stella person. How could he have betrayed her in this way? If only she could confront him with what he had done – but his mortal remains had been reduced to ashes. Death was protecting him from her desperate need to revenge herself upon him. Perhaps there was hope yet, she was still fertile, but she was hardly enthusiastic at the thought of living with another man. The idea of IVF did not appeal, and the cost at over €5,000 was way beyond what she could afford.

She hoped she would manage to transfer to the young souls for whom she would be responsible some inspiration, some creativity and some understanding of the invaluable world of art. Her thoughts turned to oil-paint and turps and brushes and suddenly she feared another panic attack. Thankfully, it did not come. This time she would not actually be doing any painting herself. She would just be instructing and directing those children towards the discovery of the magical world of shapes and shades and colours. It was so very different from what she had been doing.

She had spent her entire morning in the Prefecture Office and although hungry she really did not have the time for any serious cooking. She decided to make a quick spaghetti with pesto. It was such a good thing that she was growing fresh basil in that pot right outside the kitchen door. Now she needed to gather all the ingredients: basil leaves, olive oil, garlic pine nuts, and grated Parmigianino cheese. She put them into the blender and revelled in the sweet but somewhat sharp smell. Living could again be pleasant and promising through such simple little things. The prospect of a job, and a spaghetti al pesto with fresh basil when she was hungry, were enough to make life worthwhile.

A wave of melancholy passed over her as she thought how sad it was that she did not have someone to share this simple meal with. But thinking of the times she had cooked for Panos, sadness evaporated, giving way to bitterness.

She went over to her desk and switched on the laptop. Ah, the Internet sometimes took ages in this remote area. Several minutes elapsed and patience was running low, but at last she was able to see that she had mail. Surprisingly that poet, Nigel, to whom she had written, had sent a reply. She had not really expected that. She was curious to see what he might have written.

In his message he said that he was no longer working, which meant he might well be over fifty. That surprised her a little. From his poetry she would have thought that he was in his late twenties, although to be truthful it bore the lyrical mood of an earlier era. Yet his poems teemed with a spark of spirit that she would have attributed to a relatively young man. But then she was being unfair, what had age got do with it?

She liked the fact that he had not tried to conceal his disappointment about the mental defeat that he had suffered, it took some balls to admit that to a stranger. And behind those words of his she could feel a kind of warmth that seemed to her to go beyond pure politeness.

Anna's thoughts were interrupted by the electronic melody of her mobile. It was Ellie.

"Hey there, pretty thing, how are you doing?" Ellie was brimming with cheerfulness.

"Fine, beautiful," said Anna. That was an exchange of light-hearted flattery they had not tired of greeting each other with. Of course, as the years went by, it had also become something of a joke between them. Anna could not help a faint smile every time she heard those words, for even though they were both still good looking for their age, and most men would say they were still very desirable, she could recall how she and Ellie had looked some twenty years ago, when they really were 'pretty things'.

"Actually, today has been a really happy day, I've had some good news."

"Is it the job?" said Ellie. "Come on, do tell me. Have they called you for the teaching post?"

"Well, they didn't exactly call me, I went to them, and my back is still suffering for it, but yeah, I'm starting really soon." She was bubbling with joy and, perhaps, a kind of timid pride.

"That's great news, girl! Well done! So, this calls for a celebration! I was actually calling you to ask you if you had any special plans for the weekend?"

Ellie said this mockingly, for unless something quite extraordinary had happened such as winning the lottery or meeting Prince Charming mounted upon a white horse, there was no way Anna would have special plans for this or any other weekend.

"Hmm, I'm not sure, let me check my diary...."

Ellie laughed. "I'm coming to see you this weekend, and... I'm bringing somebody."

"A he?"

"Yes, of course!"

"What do you think you are doing?"

"Matchmaking."

"I don't need matchmaking – anyway that's ridiculously old-fashioned."

"Well you need to meet people, think men, think relationship, think sex."

"Hey, you are talking to a nearly forty-year-old widow. I should be wearing black for the rest of my life and not cavorting about with you and stray men."

"Stop sounding like a dried-up old spinster, Annoula! He's just a colleague whom I find very amusing and I thought it would be a nice change if we had some distraction and didn't have to spend our time together recounting our various misfortunes once again!" Ellie sounded both decided and convincing, and Anna could not come up with a serious argument against her plan. Anyway, she might well be right.

So, this was this indeed a good day, she thought. It was as if spring had arrived early, promising prospects and hope that she felt within her like the scented soft breeze of a sunny April day. She needed a coffee and put the small briki on the stove with water, coffee and a teaspoonful of sugar. She watched the pan carefully and when the coffee started to 'work' she stirred it. Another minute and she removed the bubbles (the 'cream') and put them in her small cup. Finally the coffee boiled again and she poured it into the cup.

She took the coffee to her desk and lit a cigarette. She had given up smoking four years ago but had relapsed after Panos' death. She did not regret it. She looked at her computer screen that had now gone black, reverting to stand-by mode. She hit the spacebar and Nigel's message reappeared. She read it once more and then clicked on 'Reply':

Dear Nigel,

It was quite a surprise to see that you've answered my mail. I am glad you did.

Thank you for your compliment on my fluency in English, I always dread that I might make some silly mistake! Being around on the site has helped to refresh my memory, as it's been quite some time since I last spoke English with somebody. Having said that it is a language I love very much.

I'm sorry to disappoint you, but I cannot say that I write anything like decent poetry, and I fear that I am far from being able to call myself a poet. I'm afraid my attempts are no better than a few clumsy scribbles as I occasionally experiment with verse. And that relates to my poetic efforts in Greek. I guess that my attempts to write poetry in English are a good deal worse! My experience and involvement in the creative arts had, until very recently, been through my painting, which I have now given up, finally and forever.

Whereabouts do you live in England? I hope that is not too intrusive a question? I live on an island, over a hundred kilometres North of Athens, but I suppose if I told you the name of the village it would sound Greek to you! I'm pretty much aware of the main regions in England.

I'm afraid I've become too talkative. I hope I haven't bored you. I would be glad to hear from you, if you feel like staying in touch.

Best Wishes,

Anna

(Lake District, UK)

Contrary to Nigel's expectations, his reputation as a poet seemed to have been enhanced over the past twenty-four hours. He was surprised by this but was not going to fool himself into imagining that he had suddenly become a better poet. He was well aware that his time in the limelight would not last.

The morning post had also brought a very fulsome letter from the CEO of the Caesar Charleston Foundation apologising for any distress caused to Nigel and enclosing their cheque for £250. He wondered whether Nigel would be prepared to go on local television along with himself.

Nigel rang the organisation and spoke to the man. "Thank you so much for the apology, it really wasn't be necessary, after all it was hardly your fault."

"We feel responsible, but what do you think of coming on local television with me. It might put things in a better light."

"I don't think so. I'm sorry but whilst I'm happy to express my thoughts about poetry either through its own medium or through prose I'm very wary of appearing on the box."

He had tried to have a conversation with Judith about his sudden change in fortune, but she was having none of it. Today she was on a 'high' and woe betide anything or anybody, most particularly poetically inclined husbands, that got in her way. Perhaps it was fortunate that the focus of her attention this morning was the garden. It was inanimate and was able to repair itself fairly easily, given time, from any wild excess on Judith's part. She had got it into her head that the small beck that ran along the western boundary could be diverted to form what she called a 'water feature'. Nigel did not altogether disapprove of the idea. "Steady on though, this will need careful planning, we had better not rush things."

Just over an hour later a van from Lakes Landscaping was outside the house, a mini digger had churned itself through what had, until recently, been a rather fine rose-bed, and Judith was leaping about directing operations. Nigel decided that the damage involved would be repairable, the price affordable and his wife impossible. He sighed, turned from the window and returned to his desk.

Emboldened by the turn of events since yesterday, he decided that he could now risk replacing the phone to its cradle so that it might fulfil its proper purpose. This it duly did, with phone calls from well-wishers keeping him busy for much of the morning. He was really quite shaken by the positive reaction that he was receiving. Perhaps it had been worth making such a bloody fool of himself. Every time his thoughts returned to that evening he felt a warm flush of embarrassment, but hell, his behaviour was almost excusable, the whole thing had been so awful. He remembered what Anna had said to him, that she felt those oafs that had jeered at him were the ones that were really in need of sympathy. The more he thought about it the more he became convinced that she was right.

Nigel took a call from the news editor of 'Poets Pages'. Would he be prepared to do an interview this very afternoon about his poetry? Yes, it had to be this afternoon because deadlines were looming. Thus it was that shortly after lunch Nigel found himself ensconced in his den with a charming, middle-aged lady who had told him her name was Angela. She was holding a somewhat anachronistic short-hand notebook and wielding a fearsome-looking pencil. He was strangely relieved that he was not being subjected to an interview that was being digitally recorded. Angela was asking him questions that were verging upon the personal.

"Why are you a poet, Nigel?"

"We all have that within us that needs to find expression. People find fulfilment in diverse ways – I don't know – fishing, racing cars, cooking. For me it is words, I have always loved playing with words and allowing them to express that which is inside me."

"So why poetry rather than prose?"

"Two reasons I suppose. First that it comes really easily to me. Secondly, and more importantly, is the rigour of poetry. The way you have to distil what you are saying into so few words. Every single word counts in a way that is not quite so essential in prose – unless of course you are writing frightfully highbrow Lit Fic."

"But you have come to writing rather late in life."

"True. I have had a worthwhile career and now that I have more time to allow some freedom to my creative side . . ."

At that moment the door opened. Judith stood stock still look-ing from one to the other of them, swaying ever so slightly.

"Floozie!" She said.

"Err – Angela, may I introduce you to me wife, Judith."

Judith was having none of it. She advanced upon the unfortunate woman and speaking slowly as if in total command of herself said, "I know what you have been up to. I will not stand for it in my home. You may leave my house now."

"I am so sorry," said Angela, "you really are mistaken, I am just talking to your husband about . . ."

Judith interrupted, "Please do not make excuses, at least not to me. I would be most grateful if you would leave. Now!"

Nigel took his wife by the hand in an attempt to lead her away from Angela, but was brushed away as if he were little more than an irritating fly. 'Oh God', he thought, why is this happening to me, and just when I have a chance to say something worthwhile about my poetry. Why does she want to spoil everything that I ever do?' He knew that there was little point in arguing with his wife. In the state she was in the only option he had was to get Angela quickly and safely out of the house. Angela was in any case already in full retreat. "

I'm so sorry," he called to her over Judith's head, "my wife isn't quite herself today."

Judith turned and gave him a look that would wither a stand-up comedian in a working men's club. "I want this Floozie out of my house. You have flung her in my face – trying as ever to tell me that I am not good enough for you."

Angela made a further despairing attempt to pacify the lady of the house, but faltered after her first few words, fixed as she was by a contemptuous glare.

The luckless journalist was ushered firmly to the front door. This time she made as if to say something to Nigel, but saw the look in Judith's eyes, turned and walked to her car. Marston's both were left standing together upon the front step nursing individual feelings of hurt and anger.

A burning sense of resentment swept over Nigel. He was, intellectually, aware that this was a different Judith to the one that he had married, but drink had done its worst to her and he felt a real black anger at being treated the way that he had been. He was also worried about what Angela would be thinking, and dared not even consider what would appear in print in 'Poets Pages'.

The small blue car disappeared up the drive. Nigel turned to his wife, his cheeks aflame and his voice half an octave higher than its normal register, "what the hell did you have to do that for?"

Judith was now all sweetness and reason. She spoke as if she were calming an hysterical child. "Now you know that you shouldn't have brought that woman here, Nige, it was a bit naughty of you wasn't it now? Never mind, I know you are sorry, just say: 'sorry Judith', and then we can forget all about it."

"Blast it! She was interviewing me for her magazine. You behaved abominably. I have no idea what I can do now to put it right."

"Don't worry, my dear, I am sure that naughty woman won't come back. It's all over now."

"I suppose I had better send her some flowers or something, along with a little note of apology from us both."

"If you want to send flowers to your little playmate then so be it – but don't you dare include my name if you write to that floozie." And with that Judith turned on her heel and stalked fairly steadily back towards the gaping hole in her lawn, every inch the wronged wife.

Nigel waited a good half-minute pondering his misfortune, but also the greater misfortune that had descended upon his wife. He turned into the house and the recently invaded sanctuary of his den. He sat down again at his desk and this time deployed the Johnny Walker. He took a satisfying gulp, and then another. The fiery liquid seemed to cool the rage and shame that he was experiencing. Judith was getting worse, he could not doubt that, although for most of the time she just appeared to be a little withdrawn. He was only too aware that the stopgap solution that he was applying to his own jangled nerves was that which was now rampant in his wife. A wave of guilt overwhelmed him. He had married Judith without really understanding what love was. His reasons for doing so seemed now to be blurred by the passing years, but he was fairly sure that she had, at least in those early days, been really rather fond of him. Nigel was a man who knew himself. He was all too well aware that 'love' had passed him by. The very last thing he needed was self-psychoanalysis, but he was all too familiar with how his early childhood had moulded him and cast him as the flawed individual that he now was. It was a place that he did not wish to revisit.

He drained his glass, wiped it with a rather crumpled cloth, and returned it to his drawer. He felt a pang of concern about his drinking. Late afternoon it might be, but this was not 'social drinking', it was the taking of a tonic to steady the nerves and he was just a bit frightened of what he was doing to himself. Perhaps Johnny Walker should indeed 'Keep Walking' and not reside so temptingly in this drawer of his desk. He had seen it not just in his wife, but in more than one good friend, alcohol in sensible quantity was wonderfully relaxing – but it could also be dangerously addictive. He needed to watch himself.

The iMac pinged for the umpteenth time; his mailboxes were demanding his attention. There was a lot of congratulatory stuff from fellow poets regarding the award, also some referring to the 'Affair at The Grand', most of which offered him sympathy. As he read them he became more and more detached from what these no doubt well-wishing people were saying. Nevertheless his inbred English politeness took over and he answered each correspondent with such courtesy as was demanded.

Another ping, and his 'Personal – Poetry' mailbox was showing a new post. He thought he had finished. Oh well he had better do this one as well otherwise it would only be first on tomorrow's list. His posture stiffened; this was interesting. The message was a further note from Anna. He read her email with care, paused and read it again. He was almost certain that this woman was saying more than she was actually writing. She did not seem to want to get involved in an in-depth discussion of his poetry, like the few 'fans' that communicated with him did, nor was she obviously trying to rope him into some sort of organization or society. Perhaps she just needed a friend? Good, from the little that she had said she seemed an interesting person, one who might provide him with some gentle intellectual stimulation. He wondered how to pitch what he wanted to say:

> *Dear Anna,*
>
> *I want to tell you that your email has touched me. As you may imagine everyone has been offering me sympathy, except you – and I reckon that makes you a rather special sort of person?*
>
> *You ask me where I live. OK, I'll tell you about that, and just a little about myself – but only on the condition that you do the same for me.*
>
> *I live in the Northwest of England, an area we call the Lake District. I am probably a bit prejudiced but I have to tell you it is the prettiest mountain scenery in the British Isles, although our highest Fells (that's what we call mountains) are lower than those in Scotland, or even Wales. I live with my wife of many years in what used to be an old farmhouse, long and low, with very thick stone walls. It is painted off-white like so many traditional houses in these*

parts. Tell me how different that is from the sort of house that you live in.

I have more or less retired from business now that I have just reached my fifties. I don't feel quite that old – unless I go for a very long walk when bits of me start to creak!

Retirement has allowed me to get more involved in the things that I love, but have rather missed out on earlier in life, including poetry. I live a rather dull life here. My wife is not as well as she should be and for some time we have led somewhat separate lives, but we have two wonderful grown-up children who both live miles away. Do you have a family?

You said in your note to me that you hoped that you had not 'tired' me by writing. Far from it, it is only boring people that tire me, and that is hardly a description of you, so please write again.

Fondly
Nigel

He sat and read his e-mail through very carefully. Was he going too far? He felt a definite tingle of affinity for this Anna, but why that should be he had no idea. Nigel was not one who felt comfortable exploring his emotions, his introspection being satiated by poetic musings. At heart he knew himself to be an uptight Englishman who was only prepared to expose his inner thoughts on his own terms, and that to him nowadays meant through poetry. He toyed with that half full bottle of whisky in his drawer and smiled to himself as he recognized his own optimistic nature in not thinking of it as half empty. No, it was not needed now. False courage was the last thing that he required.

He wondered about leaving the sending of that email until tomorrow. Sometimes things could look very different after a night's sleep. Perhaps he should turn over in his mind the consequences of getting into a friendly correspondence with someone he had never met. No, bugger it, after all he was an Aries, and Aries are always certain in their decisions. If he was about to make a big mistake then he would just have to get himself out of whatever mess he found himself in.

He half closed his eyes, screwed his face up, and hit the Send button. There was a satisfying 'Whoosh' as his mail left the safety of his desktop and winged its way to Greece.

5

(Evia, Greece)

Anna opened her eyes with a feeling of bliss still very vivid, almost overwhelmingly present, and she was reluctant to let it go. The dream was recurring more frequently now, perhaps once a week. Her subconscious would skip bits and insert bits according to its own unfathomable rules but there was usually a progression from deep anxiety to serenity and contentment. That revelatory view of the blue sky, was so much in contrast with the feelings of anxiety and futility that permeated through the early stages. She struggled to explain the wonderful feeling that she had experienced, but then she feared that she might destroy its magical joy by dissecting it, just as the beauty of a wild animal is destroyed on a laboratory table.

There was an intense burst of bird song from outside her window, and she realized for the first time just how many birds there were around this house. Perhaps they had even made their nests in the roof. She left her bed and headed for the kitchen. She normally had a light breakfast, a glass of milk or some yoghurt with fruit, but today she had this feeling of fullness. It was not with food, she hadn't had any, it was rather a pleasant, sweet echo of her dream that she could not get out of her mind. All she needed was a cup of coffee. She took it outside into the yard. The weather had changed at last and was now compensating for its previous behaviour by providing a warm, sunny day. She sat in the sunshine, smelling the fine breeze that bore an early, faint scent of budding wildflowers and herbs. Spring was indeed close.

The electronic, somewhat brisk, but happy tune of her mobile sent Anna inside, uncertain for a few moments as to where on earth she had put it down. It was Lukas.

"Hi, little sister, how are you my love?" Lukas had always called her 'little sister'.

"Fairly well, my hero. Right now I'm enjoying the glorious sunshine that has arrived at last. What's the weather like in Athens?"

"It is trying to be sunny but not making much of a job of it."

"Lukas, I'm so excited, I've got a job!"

"That's great! Is that teaching post you went for?"

"Yes, and guess what, I'm starting in just a few days' time."

"I'm so happy for you, well done my girl."

"So, what's the news from the capital?" said Anna, though what she was really asking for was Lukas' own news.

"I thought I'd drop by to see how my little's sister's doing. That is if you'll treat me to a nice cup of coffee. I don't expect it will take me more than an hour and a half to get to you."

"You drive too fast"

"So you are always telling me."

"Anyway, baby brother it's a lovely surprise and of course it would be great to see you, but aren't you working today?" Surely it wasn't a public holiday that she had forgotten about.

"Yeah, of course I am, I mean I normally would be, but today I just didn't feel like it so I took a sickie."

This sounded most unlike Lukas, after cars and speed his obsession was his job, it always had been. He worked at the creative department of a big advertising company and it had taken him years of sleepless nights and whole-hearted devotion to climb his way up through the ranks to his current post of deputy project manager. He had his heart set on the project manager position, and she knew that he was not the sort of person to pull a sick note unless he really was ill.

"OK, honey, I'll be waiting for you, but please, make it at least two hours."

"All right, all right, you don't need to tell me about my driving again."

What on earth was she to do about lunch. Lukas was hardly going to drool over the simple meal of lentils that she had cooked the previous day. However the first thing that needed doing was to deal with that online order for the English poetry books that she wanted. The computer came to life and her home page appeared bringing up her emails. Nigel had sent another message. She was glad to see it. It was like a view from or into another world, and she could not deny the pleasurable vibes that resounded within her. She read it a bit too fast. Nigel had previously shown a delightful, but rather reserved, sort of detached politeness, but here he was displaying a different mood. Now he seemed more loosened up, warmer and more per-sonal, as if he was really interested in her life, and her country. Yes, she thought in some bitterness, this country of ours that has become the freak-show of the circus. Now the whole world can gawp at us and prod us to see if we might growl.

She supposed she could just afford a minute or two to send a short email to Nigel before she started to prepare the meal of beef stewed in lemon sauce and mashed potatoes that Lukas loved so much.

Dear Nigel,
I'm so glad to hear from you! It is a pleasant sur-
prise to know that we seem to be such like-minded people.

No, there's nothing really special about me, I'm just an ordinary getting on for 40-year-old Greek woman, with an inclination to the creative arts, but who has produced little of real worth other than a painting or two. On the other hand, I suppose that we're all special in some way, aren't we?

I know of the Lake District, it is said to be very beautiful indeed, although, unfortunately, I have never had the chance of seeing that for myself.

As I told you, I live in a village, or to be more precise, just on the outskirts of it. It is on the island of Evia – which is hardly a real island as there are two bridges to it from the mainland. It's a very beautiful place too. Although I have owned this small house for ages, I've been living here for only the past few months.

I've got a lovely garden and some nice views of both the mountains and of the sea, the latter is close enough to be able to walk to it for a swim, but when it is really hot I usually take the car.

I am recently widowed and have no children. I lived in England for a few months rather more than 20 years ago. I was based in London where I did a short course at The Slade. I am not sure if it did that much for my art, but at least my English improved!

She paused and read Nigel's message again. He said he was married, although there was that concern about his wife's health. She wondered what the problem was. He talked about his children, *that pang again.* What was she supposed to say? If she dared tell him how things really were with her, he would return a letter of sympathy or, even worse, pity. Well, it seemed that apart from poetry, they had another thing in common: neither wished for sympathy. She decided to skip that.

> *I have given up painting now, although I have just had my application accepted for the post of a surrogate art teacher at the local high school. It'll be something totally new for me.*
>
> *What did you do for a living? And how do you feel about this change in your routine now that you are at least partly retired? Do you travel at all? Have you ever been to Greece?*
>
> *Wow, that was rather a barrage of questions! You can answer only those you want to!*
>
> *I really must close now. I hope you write back soon. I find your emails strangely comforting.*
>
> *Fondly,*
> *Anna*

Glancing at the clock on her computer she realised that Lukas would be almost half way to her by now. Whoops, she had been wasting precious time emailing rather than getting on with the job in hand. She would like to get at least most of the cooking done by the time Lukas arrived. Guiltily she switched off the computer. There were other important things to think about now.

She washed the meat, cut the onions and sautéed them in olive oil until they became light brown.

There had been no time to revise that email, she just hoped that she had not made a terrible mistake, a stupid spelling inaccuracy or a grammatical error.

She turned the meat from side to side so it didn't get burnt, added the carrots, salt, pepper and spice, and four leaves of bay.

She should have started this cooking ages ago, why did she always put herself under such stress?

She would add the lemon along with just a little flour towards the end. She put the potatoes in the saucepan to boil.

Once again that order for poetry books had remained unsent.

Lukas was ringing the bell already. He feigned a nonchalant smile, but he hugged her for a little bit longer and just a shade tighter than he usually did. It added to that nagging fear that she had felt when he had phoned her. Clearly something was greatly troubling him. He took a seat, complimented her on how well she looked, and asked her about her newly acquired job.

This was not the first time Lukas had visited her following her move so it was a surprise to her when he started wandering around the living room, commenting on the surroundings.

Anna made coffee and, filling two cups, waved him towards the sofa and took a seat opposite him. She stared at him persistently so that Lukas averted his eyes. A few minutes passed in silence with neither of them drinking any coffee.

Finally he spoke. "Everything is screwed up, They have bloody well gone and fired me ". He looked utterly crushed.

This was not as bad as she had feared, it was not that she did not understand what his career meant to him, but given the way he looked, she had dreaded that it might have been something worse.

"Oh" she said and then paused.

She didn't want to smother him with shallow encouragement, an everything-is- going-to-be-all right pat on the back. She realised what it meant to lose something important. She knew that the chances of Lukas finding a similar job here were almost non-existent. She understood what this meant to him after all those years of effort and hard, conscientious work. It was as if he had bet everything on the favourite, and it had failed to win.

"What are you going to do?" If she did not do sympathy, neither did Lukas.

"I'm going to leave"

"What do you mean, leave? Where are you going?" This was not what she wanted to hear.

"I'm going to France," he said, lowering his tone, as if he was afraid of his own words.

"France? What will you do there, for God's sake you don't speak a single word of French?"

"I'll learn. I'm a fast learner. A guy at work, who got fired long before me, has found a job there. There are lots of jobs available that would be just right for me. I'll have to start from the bottom again, I know that, but at least I'll have a chance."

He sounded, and looked, very sad but equally he was clearly resolute. It would be futile to try to dissuade him from doing something he had decided on so firmly, she knew her brother. Apart from that, there really was hardly anything that could be said to him about it. Much as it broke her heart to know that he was going to be so far away, she knew he was doing the only thing that he possibly could do for his own good.

"You will make it," she said getting up and heading towards the kitchen. "Let's eat, and celebrate your new life."

The meal had turned out well, but Anna knew that, like her, Lukas was struggling to put a brave face on the situation. They drank some wine; they attempted light conversation on inconsequential matters; they failed. The air became suffocated with a toxic silence that seemed set to stay with them. Lukas held her by the hand and stroked it.

"Don't worry little sister, everything is going to turn out just fine." He smiled at her and Anna made a huge effort not to cry.

"Do Mum and Dad know?"

"Yes, but I've spun them a bit of a tale. I told them that the company has opened a new office in France and that I'll be promoted to project manager back here on condition that I help with the organisation of the new French branch."

So, both Lukas and she had become masters of making up fanciful stories to protect their parents. But this was at least one less worry. The knowledge that Lukas was emigrating would have caused them to sink into the deepest of melancholy.

"I'll come and help you with packing."

"No, darling, I've already done most of that, and I want to leave that apartment with the notion that it was just a place where I spent a casual couple of years of my life. You packing with me would make me think of it so differently, besides I'm really not up to the emotional stress of parting from you like that."

"So you have already packed? Are you leaving so soon?" she could not keep the despair out of her voice.

"Exactly two weeks from now. The apartment already looks bare and deserted, and I haven't cleaned for some time, so I suppose I'll have to spend the next fifteen days living in rather primitive conditions. But this will just reinforce that last memory I was talking about." He had clearly put a lot of effort in trying to hide his real feelings.

"And why didn't you tell me about it sooner? Why did you wait to the last minute? I must be about the last person to know."

"I know it'll sound stupid to you, but I really didn't know how to tell you. You've been through so much, so fucking much, that I didn't want to dump yet another worry upon you! So I just thought I might save you a bit if I put off telling you . . ." He could not go on.

"That was pretty silly you know. People that love each other are here for the rainy days as well as the fine ones." But there was no need to go any further; Lukas seemed to have had all he could take.

"I'll come to Athens to see you off at the airport."

"Oh no, don't do that. I can't guarantee I won't cry if I see you standing there waving at me. Besides, it will be a working day for you! You can come and visit me in France as soon as I'm settled."

They walked together to the door. She looked at this much-loved brother of hers. his slim tall silhouette, his light brown hair, his greenish-brown eyes, and his nose that bent slightly to the left after a punch from a fight over a girl when he was at school.

"I'll send you my address and everything as soon as I get there. Come on, haven't you always wanted to see Paris?" It was his way of finding a cheerful way to end their conversation.

Anna hugged him hard, compensating for all the hugs that she would miss from him, all the embraces that she would not be able to give him for a very long time. She was practised now at holding back tears, she concentrated on the chances that he might have in France, for in Greece there was no chance for him at all. At least he would avoid the misery and self-doubt that would come with unemployment. He was such a creative young man, surely he would manage to make something of himself, even in foreign country. She kissed him and from the very depths of her heart she wished him good luck.

(Lake District, UK)

They were not going to be terribly late. Nigel admitted to himself that he had been a bit hard on Judith when she was waving different coloured frocks at him, undecided as to what she should wear. Long ago he had learned better than to express a clear preference in such matters. The invitation for the first official sailing on the recently restored 'Pride of the Lakes' had been addressed to 'Mr & Mrs Marston', and he had replied that they would both be going. He thought rather ruefully that in the state that his wife was in she was quite capable of changing her mind right up to the very last moment.

They had hardly spoken throughout the thirty-minute journey, but now Judith turned to him." My turn to drive back," she said, "I promise to have nothing to drink. Anyway, I'm quite happy to drive back if you like. You drink, it's your occasion really."

"Thanks," said Nigel, "that's kind of you. You'd better stick to something soft. At this sort of do you can feel a bit awkward if you don't have a glass in your hand."

"I think I'll just allow myself just one glass of white wine, that'll be fine. I won't need any more, I can make it last for an hour or so if I have to."

Parking was easier than Nigel had expected. He pulled in at the end of a row of cars facing some concrete bollards. They would not have far to walk. Drinks were being handed out in the visitor kiosk as the guests made their way through to the boat, and Nigel was pleased to see that they were not alone in arriving rather late. They took a glass of different coloured wine each and walked along the wooden gangway and onto the boat. There must have been rather more than sixty people aboard, He and Judith split up and mingled with the crowd.

It was not that often that Nigel was able to drink without having to bother about driving himself home, especially from an afternoon party such as this. It was good to be able to chat amicably with people that he knew and to shake hands with some that he did not. Given that he was not going to drive home Nigel was not shy about allowing his glass to be refilled regularly. Along with all the other guests he suffered three, mercifully short, speeches that extolled the restoration and thanked those who had contributed towards it either financially or with their hard graft. Then the boat slipped away from the pier and out into the lake. The sun had now fully broken through the clouds and Nigel was swept along with the rest of the guests as the throng headed happily for the open upper deck. As he made his way up the companionway he found himself, by chance, walking up the steps with Judith.

"Hello Sailor," she said, in a voice that was rather too loud for the circumstances. Her face was a little flushed and she was steadying herself against the stair rail with her right hand. Nigel noticed that she was carrying her wine glass and that it was still about half full.

"You did say you were driving us home?"

"Course I am, bloody good driver that's what I am." And with that they reached the upper deck and Judith was quickly swept away forward in a press of people whilst Nigel made his way mid-ships.

"Hey Nigel come on up and tell us what you think of this old lady." He had known Bob Thacker, skipper of 'The Pride' for many years and did not need asking twice. The handling of a large passenger boat such as this came back to him very easily.

"She looks good, Bob, you've done a great job with her."

"Hmmm, I would have preferred something more modern, but that isn't company policy, it's all to do with promoting the right image, and they reckon we should only run historic ships."

Nigel was looking down at a gaggle of people standing by the forward rail. They seemed very animated and by their manner they must have had quite a bit to drink. Casual interest turned to a more focussed concern when he realised that it was his wife who was holding court in the middle of the group. Indeed she seemed to be the very centrepiece of the party.

"Here, Bob, take the wheel. There's something going on down there, Judith's involved and I don't quite like the look of it. I'd better go down and see what the hell she's up to this time."

"Bit of a spirited woman that wife of yours."

"She is that. Bit of a trial too, and that's the truth."

"You'd better get on down then," said Bob, taking the wheel.

"Thanks for letting me helm her, she really is OK."

Nigel slipped quickly down the near-vertical ladder from the wheelhouse to the forward deck and walked swiftly towards the bows.

Judith had by this time taken her coat off, exposing her bare arms. Her dark blue low-cut dress made the very best of her décolletage which despite her advancing age held a definite attraction, Indeed the half dozen men gathered around her were enjoying the very best of it.

"Come on then, boys," she was saying, "do you want me as your figurehead or not? No good down here on the deck, a figurehead needs to be prominent, I need to be prominent. I need to be up there. Give us a shanty or two my lads and hoist away."

"If your husband hadn't just joined us I'd give you more than a shanty!"

"Oh don't mind him – he's only a poet. Come on then . . ."

At which exhortation four of her followers jostled to hoist Judith up onto the small triangular platform on the forepeak. Judith attempted with a good measure of success to adopt the Kate Winslet posture, bending forward with her arms outstretched. The assembled company cheered loudly.

Nigel decided that things had gone far enough. His wife was swaying about, occasionally grabbing the jack-staff, and clearly in grave danger of departing the ship. "Come on Judith, that's enough, come off there."

Judith turned at his voice and stumbled slightly as her left foot caught in the starboard fairlead. She overbalanced and screamed. Steve, who was nearest to her leaped up onto the forepeak and grabbed her arm as she fell, swinging her back into the hands of the others, however the momentum of his action continued to twist him so that he missed his footing and with a cry of "Oh Shit!" fell from the very front of the boat, landing in the water on the port side.

"Man overboard, port side," shouted Nigel, pointing to port. He looked to the wheelhouse and saw Bob cranking the heavy wheel to port so as to turn the props away from the man in the water. The whistle sounded six times and a lifebuoy was thrown from the stern. Bob struggling to manoeuvre the unwieldy vessel managed, in slightly less than three minutes, to execute a Whiteman turn. He brought it to a stand heading into the light breeze just a couple of meters from the strongly-swimming Steve who was unceremoniously dragged back on board.

Nigel turned to Judith "You bloody little fool, look what you've done."

"Don't be such a stuffed-up prig," she said wriggling, for the benefit of her slightly depleted audience, rather provocatively into her jacket. "Come on boys, we need a dink,"

Back at the car they glared at each other with mutual distaste. "You said you were going to drive."

"And so I am prig-thing, so I am."

"Well I can't drive, I'm well over the limit," said Nigel.

"Well fuck you then, 'cos I want to be driven by a real man, not some wimp who can't enjoy himself."

"You can't drive, you've had more than I have. And you said that you weren't going to drink."

"That was before you were so bloody rude to me in front of all those nice people."

"Nonsense you had already had far too much well before that."

"Well sod you then, my darling husband, I am more than happy to drive you."

So saying Judith slid into the driver's seat and started the car. Nigel made to stop her, but the lady was determined. The vehicle lurched off gaining speed over some ten metres or so of tarmac before it struck one of the bollards demarcating the edge of the parking area and came to a dead halt.

"Fucking stupid place to leave a lump of concrete," said Judith, now out of the car and peering under the front to see what had arrested her progress.

In the end Nigel phoned for a taxi that, with one stop to allow Judith to throw up on the verge, delivered them back home.

By the time they reached the front door she was incapable of standing. He supported her up the stairs and half dropped her, fully dressed on the bed. He was not minded to remove her clothes at present and she seemed to have lost her shoes somewhere along the way. He closed the bedroom door and walked out on the sorry scene.

He phoned Lynn, their G.P. and recounted this latest episode. Lynn was both professional and sympathetic, She was well aware of Judith's drink problem.

"I worry," said Nigel," because she simply will not accept that she has a problem. Do you think there is anything we can do?"

"To be honest, Nigel, there is very little in the way of help that we can offer until she, herself, asks for it. It would be good to involve her with Alcoholics Anonymous, but I suppose that's an impossibility?"

"Indeed. I tried to suggest just that to her but she went absolutely wild. She denied that she was drinking any more than me and accused me of trying to get rid of her. The problem seems to be getting worse. Sometimes she lives in a world of her own and I just cannot tell if she is reacting to real things or things imagined."

The prognosis was not good. She was clearly on a steep decline into chronic alcoholism and there was no cure without her acceptance of her condition. As time went on she would become more prone to blackouts, and erratic memory loss. To Nigel this seemed like a slow death sentence, a likelihood of his wife slipping into greater and greater dissociation.

Nigel was finding the situation harder and harder to shield her erratic behaviour from their friends. There is a social stigma against the alcoholic. If only she could have been diagnosed as primarily bi-polar, or even schizoid, then it would be a great deal easier to explain that to people. This would be something their acquaintances could understand and could cope with. It would allow the social niceties to continue. To him this sad descent into alcoholism seemed to have been caused by failure. Her failure, but also his failure. He asked Lynn about medication. Perhaps there was something that could alleviate the craving for alcohol.

Previously Lynn had prescribed Disulfiam, but the effect of in-ducing vomiting when alcohol was taken had met with Judith's total refusal to have anything further to do with it. "Would you take a pill to make yourself sick?" she had asked, and with some justification.

Lynn had then rather reluctantly tried first Neltrexone, then Acomproaste. Neither had any marked effect, no doubt because they were only fully effective once the 'subject' had stopped drink-ing for several days. This was not something that Judith would even contemplate.

"Basically, Nigel, there is very little that we can do. If she could just admit the problem then I can talk to you both about possible solutions."

From the time that he and Judith had got into the taxi Nigel had been able to at least half-relax his thoughts from his present situation and allow them to wander towards a certain Greek woman whose 'presence' he was beginning to find unaccountably soothing. Silly really, he had no idea what she was like. It was just that she was a part of his life that was not contaminated by him, or Judith, or the whole rotten portion of the world that he existed in. Now he made his way down the stairs with a quickened step. With almost indecent haste he crossed to his desk and clicked on the Mac Mail icon. Yes! There was indeed a message from Anna. He read it and, perhaps in part due to the amount of wine that he had consumed, he felt a warm glow of kinship with this distant friend. Almost immediately he began to write:

> *Dearest Anna,*
>
> *Your message came as a beacon of light to my dismal evening. I have had the worst day imaginable. Nothing seems to have gone right. I am not sure if I mentioned that my wife, Judith, has something of a problem, and this can lead to fairly violent mood-swings. I find this so difficult to live with because she used to be a reasonably well-balanced person. Now I find her almost impossible to deal with. Today she very nearly killed someone by being stupid on a boat. Luckily no real harm was done except to our car which she impaled on a bollard. I suppose that I shouldn't blame her, it's probably as much my fault as hers that we seem incapable of being civil to one another, but I fear that tomorrow will be bad as well. She will get very depressed about her behaviour, and that is almost worse that when she is on a 'high'.*
>
> *Oh, Anna, I'm so sorry to burden you with my problems. You have obviously done really well to get yourself a job when it cannot be easy to do so in your country and I am really happy for you.*
>
> *In my late teens I spent a couple of weeks on one of the Greek islands, but other than that I only really know about Greece from Classical studies. That gives me a great respect for your country and your people. Without your*

ancestors there would be no democracy. I rather think that Aristotle 'retired' to Evia when he was hounded out of Athens. I wonder what it is like to live somewhere with such an ancient history.

You ask about my work. I am retired now. I have been involved with boats for the last twenty years, running my own small company that I was lucky to sell well just a couple of years ago.

Now at last I have the freedom that I want to allow myself to develop my repressed creativity. You ask about my 'change in routine'. To tell you the truth I am thriving on it. I have so much more time to do the things that I really want to do – and that of course includes writing poetry – and I have now escaped from the intense responsibility that comes with running one's own business.

I find it just a little awkward writing to you when I have no idea what you look like. I rather think that an exchange of photos would be the right thing. I hope you agree. To further this I am attaching a photo that was taken of me about nine months ago when I was applying for a new passport – it makes me look a bit grim but I daresay it is a fair likeness. I am full of hope that you will reciprocate . . .

Anna, you're a good deal younger than me, and living in a country that is far away from here and which has a very different culture. Nevertheless I feel so much closer to you than would seem appropriate given these circumstances. And I wonder if you feel this as well, or if I am just a foolish and rather stupid old man fabricating a relationship that could never exist?

Affectionately,
Nigel

This time Nigel did not want to think before he sent the message, he just hit the send button and closed his eyes. Five minutes later he went upstairs and gently undressed his soundly sleeping wife. She was wearing a bra but no knickers. He hoped, that this was through absent-mindedness rather than design. He gently tucked the duvet around the sleeping form and retired to his own bedroom.

6 |

(Evia, Greece)

Ellie's phone-call woke Anna from a troubled, anxious, but dream-free sleep. Where was the bloody phone? Surely it was on the bedside cabinet somewhere? As yet unable to open her eyes she fumbled for the home button, pressed it, and raised the mobile to her right ear. She heard Ellie's voice. A voice that sounded ridiculously cheerful for this time of the morning.

"Are you still in bed you lazy thing? We're over half way to your spot. Come on, get up and get yourself ready. We're taking you out, so the least you can do is wake up and have some nice hot coffee ready for us when we get to you." Her voice rose almost to a shriek, "Now, open your eyes and get out of that bed, immediately!"

This visit was one that Anna had looked forward to with joy and excitement, yet despite this initial anticipation she really did not want it to happen now. True it was good to be looking forward to actually doing something, and there was always the pleasure of seeing Ellie, but no, the prospect of having to meet a strange man filled her with dread this morning. This was supposed to have been a cheering-up day, a carefree get-together. Now it seemed to be nothing but a trial. But there was no way out of it, Ellie and this man were speeding this way, indeed they would have already covered most of the distance from Athens. There was no way that she could pull out of seeing them at this stage unless she wanted to be unforgivably rude, and in doing so hurt her friend. If only she had remembered yesterday that this was the day that Ellie was coming to see her she could easily have just phoned and cancelled the visit.

Every limb in her body protested as she forced herself to abandon her comfortable resting place. Her tired body was reluctant to do what she wanted of it, most particularly to crawl out of bed. She felt as if she had spent the last twelve hours digging in the heaviest of soil. Such was the reward of her troubled night.

Anna switched on the water heater; she needed to take a shower as soon as possible. It had been a whole three days since she last had one and now she felt sticky and dirty and smelly. She could barely put up with herself, so what would anyone else think of her. The water would take a while to heat up so she made herself a cup of coffee and drank it whilst she was waiting.

Once again she did not feel like having anything else for break-fast. This would be the fourth day in a row that she would have eaten nothing. Unlike that pleasant morning after she last had that dream of hers, when she did not want breakfast because she felt full of happiness, she now just could not bring herself to eat. This had happened before. She knew it was a stress-related thing. The first few months after she had moved into the cottage she had only managed the to eat a very small amount. It had taken her a lot of mental and physical effort to restore her diet to a regular three meals a day. Now it seemed that she had returned to her former state. Just for today, she thought. She would manage to put things back in order after this, for that was what she had always done; picked herself up again after a fall and got on with life.

She pulled on a pair of blue-jeans and a loose top. Her hair was still damp from the shower that had dispelled some of the tiredness that she felt deep inside her. It was as if it had been washed away by the hot water that she had allowed to pour over her body for so long.

And now the doorbell was ringing and she could hear Ellie twittering and giggling outside the house. She managed a cheerful smile as she opened the door and Ellie rushed in giving Anna a warm, tight hug and a friendly kiss on her cheek. "I've missed you, silly" she said, taking a step back and freeing Anna, who was now able to see the stranger who still stood on the door-step a trifle awkwardly. obviously waiting for Ellie to introduce him. "Oh, and this is Stergios" she said with a kind of cheerful embarrassment.

Stergios was slim and rather short. He had brown eyes and his hair was a little longer than one would consider usual for a lawyer. It was just beginning to grey, in a manner that Anna found quite attractive. However nothing could dispel her unhappy concern that Ellie had brought this Stergios to meet her under an inappropriate notion of matchmaking. She found the very idea of allowing a man into her life faintly repulsive, particularly if said man was clearly being forced upon her. She could not come to terms with the vehemence of her rejection and sought logical reasons. Stergios was short, way shorter than the 1.75 metres that she had always considered the 'cut off point' for a suitable partner. She admitted to herself that this was prejudiced and unreasonable. Furthermore it was a case of rejecting another human being on grounds of their physical appearance. She was not happy with herself.

Stergios smiled warmly and extend his hand in a gesture of friendship. "Pleased to meet you Anna," he said reinforcing his warm smile. She returned the handshake and his greeting but was, despite her efforts to be civil, unable to manage more than the briefest of half-smiles.

There was an awkward silence.

Ellie was already in the house.

"Please, do come in" she said finally, allowing sufficient space for him to enter. "I didn't make coffee, despite my friends demands, as I did not know if you prefer Greek coffee?".

"Don't worry," he said, "Whatever is easiest for you."

"Okay, Greek coffee then for both of you. It's a small thank you for driving all this way."

"Just being here in this lovely place and in good company is thanks enough for me."

"Do sit down and make yourself comfortable" said Anna as she scooped up the cup with the remains of her morning coffee and headed for the kitchen, "and how to you like your coffee, Stergios?"

"Μετριω." He said, indicating a liking for at least a little sugar,

"Just make it quick" shouted Ellie, "as I said, we're going to take you out for lunch today".

"Would you rather we sat in the yard?" Anna asked as she approached them with the tray containing three double cups of Greek coffee. Ellie was a confirmed smoker and from what she could gather from the packet of cigarettes on the coffee table in front of Stergios, he was as well. Although Anna had started smoking again she really did not like the smell of smoke and quite definitely did not like it in her house. She felt lucky that a faint sun had just come out. It made sitting outdoors tolerable, especially as the weather looked as if it was going to get even better. Ellie was quick to stand up and exclaim, "That's good idea!", partly because she actually preferred being outdoors but also because she knew of Anna's dislike of the smell of smoking.

They sat and sipped their coffee and cold water. Ellie kept talking incessantly, updating Anna on all the news on every possible matter; job situation, common friends, just a little of her personal life, the politico-economic developments as she perceived them, new films she had liked, a notable painting exhibition. Ellie must have felt nervous, for she always spoke too much when she was unsure of herself or her situation.

Anna was happy to just let her rattle on, it covered any mild embarrassment that she felt about being subjected to this man. Stergios, for his part, was almost silent. He seemed totally relaxed and unpretentious. Anna did not know if she liked him being so laid-back in the house of a woman he had only just met, accompanied by another who was not exactly a close friend either. But then again, would she really have liked a stiff, reserved kind of a stranger sitting in her yard? Perhaps the best thing she could do was just relax as well.

Coffee over, they drove to a coastal taverna that Anna knew was open all-year-round. In the summer there were tables out front on the beach so that customers could enjoy the view and the soothing, rhythmical sound that the wavelets made on the sand as they splashed gently against the shore. Today the sun was shining and becoming ever brighter as the few remaining clouds were chased away, but the only outside tables at this time of the year were in the small garden facing the street. It was pleasant sitting here with, in contrast to the summer months, so few people about. There was only one other group of customers in the place.

Stergios proved to be a very good company. He was a man of many interests, quite humorous at times, and some of his views were fairly radical. Not what she would have expected from a lawyer thought Anna, and then reproached herself for being so prejudiced, for Ellie herself was a lawyer, although she hardly resembled the rest of her kind. And, contrary to his quieter demeanour in the house, Stergios was anything but shy or unforthcoming. She found his conversation interesting as he comfortably passed from one topic to another, and at times he was really very amusing. She supposed the tsipouro they had all indulged themselves in had helped in that. He told her that he was 48, divorced with two grown-up daughters.

He had chosen to work in the public sector - that, she thought, might well explain to a large degree his somewhat unconventional style. Apparently, when he had applied for law school, the idea of practising as a private lawyer did not chime with his slightly unconventional views. He said the public sector had left him with much more room to be himself.

The conversation flowed unhurriedly. They discovered that they had a lot of common interests and shared the same views on many of the issues they discussed. Ellie was not as talkative anymore, and was now drifting happily in and out of the conversation whilst Anna found herself fully engaged with it, to such an extent that she completely forgot her troubles. Furthermore she was really becoming quite flattered by the way Stergios was giving her his full attention. She liked the way he looked deep in her eyes as they talked, the way he focused on her while managing not to be neglectful or impolite to Ellie.

On occasion, perhaps when making a particular point, he would touch Anna's hand or arm, a gesture he repeated for a more prolonged time on a couple of further occasions. Anna did not withdraw from this. Perhaps it was because of her wish not to spoil the pleasant atmosphere, or because of the tsipouro, or the fact that she had missed human contact for so long. Or it might just have been that she had started, fully against her earlier intentions to take just something of a liking to this man.

It was late afternoon. The sun was already setting and it was getting really chilly sitting outside. Ellie and Stergios both had to work the next day and they faced the best part of a two-hour drive back home to Athens. Ellie called for the bill, paid it, and then left the two of them alone together with the somewhat feeble excuse that she had better take advantage of the toilets here so that they wouldn't need to stop on the way back home.

Stergios took out a pen and a professional card and wrote down his mobile phone number. He opened Anna's hand and placed the card in it. He said "Call me, I can be here in no time. I would like to think that I could have a further opportunity to enjoy the benefit both your conversation as well as your physical presence," He smiled, and looked at her meaningfully. Anna looked at him and said nothing. She took the card and thrust it in her bag just as Ellie was taking her seat back at the table.

Back at the house Ellie gave Anna a long, warm embrace and said "You will take care of yourself, won't you? I shall be back to see you the first chance I get. Get ready for that job next week, you have to make sure those kids are enchanted, but I know you will. I'm not wishing good luck yet, I'll call you." Anna stood for a few seconds and waved as the car turned the corner in the road and the car containing her two friends sped away.

She turned back into her house, took a few logs and lit the fire. She could do with a cigarette. The smoke should be drawn in the direction of the fire and so up the chimney. As she took the packet out of her bag, she accidentally caught hold of Stergios' card along with the cigarettes. She looked at it. What should she do? He was a pleasant enough man and a good companion, but there was something wrong. With a gut-wrenching sense of despair, she realised that it was not Stergios that was 'wrong', but herself. She had no appetite for such a relationship. However much she might enjoy good conversation felt unable to face the inevitable psychological and physical stages of a relationship with this man, pleasant as he undoubtedly was. Her yearning for fulfilment needed more than this, more of a challenge, more of a struggle.

For nearly a minute she stood still, her feelings wavering between acceptance and rejection or perhaps a combination of the two. She closed her eyes. That dream plucked meaningfully at her heart. She threw Stergios' card into the now blazing fire. She lit a cigarette, then sat down at her desk and switched on her computer. She had forgotten once again to place that mail order for the poetry books. With a start of guilt she remembered Nigel. Perhaps he had sent a reply?

He had indeed. At its sight she felt a kind of satisfaction or even glee that she could not easily explain. She indulged in the words, the sentences and the paragraphs that were neatly arranged before her on the screen. She recognised a feeling of warmth spreading within her as she read about his life, his political views, and his kind comment that her emails were of some importance to him. It was not so much the words that he wrote that had this warming effect upon her. If she thought logically about it, this e-mail although more personal than the previous one, was little more than a friendly update. And yet, the kind of intimacy she felt as she read it was more than strange to her. Her stomach tightened when she got to the part where he had asked her about her family status. She should have expected that, after all he had shared information with her that he could hardly have found easy or pleasant to recount. She wondered if he was used to being so open with people. He certainly hadn't given her that sort of impression.

It wasn't until she had read the e-mail for a second time that she realised she had overlooked the attachment. She clicked on it, and suddenly Nigel appeared in front of her face. Wow! He was rather more handsome than she had imagined, but his hair a little greyer. It was so good that she now knew what he looked like, and she hurried to take a photo of herself, which took her several attempts before she was satisfied that she did not look too awful.

> *Dearest Nigel,*
> *Thank you so much for the photo. Yes, I entirely agree, it*
> *is an excellent idea to be able to see what we look like – and*

I am attaching a shot that I have just taken of myself. It took me three goes before I managed to take one that did not make me look like the Wicked Witch of the West.

It's so strange that you close your message with the very question that I have been asking myself for the past few days. And by doing so it is as if you are confirming that this closeness must be true, not just a product of our imagination.

You shouldn't worry about burdening me with your problems. The way that I see things the sharing of personal worries is what friendship is about. Actually, I think it is very brave of you to trust me with things so close to your heart.

I am so sorry to hear you had such a bad day and also about your wife... What is she suffering from? Isn't there any sort of treatment for her condition? I imagine it must be very hard to live with somebody with whom you can't communicate anymore. It seems to me that this would be one of the most intolerable situations I could find myself in. I think lack of communication could drive me crazy, but then again, I can understand how somebody can gradually be led into it and perhaps get used to it. I'm so sorry, it is as if I'm saying that I pity you for what you're going through, which is not true at all. I fully understand that this is just one part of your life.

Happy as I am about the teaching position that I've been appointed to, I know that it's only a short-term one. I've only been accepted as a surrogate, which means I'm left without a job as soon as the academic year is over. In my case, this means just three and half months of work. Whether I'll be re-hired or not, is very much in the lap of The Gods.

On my family status Nigel, I used to be married but am no longer so. I have no children, although it was something that I wanted very much. But it seems life has its own rules and much as we might question some of its decisions, we can do no more than abide by them. I realise this sounds sort of fatalistic and it probably is. Perhaps it's my scepticism about the choices that we are presented with and my belief that we should have it within ourselves to recognise and grab every chance while it is there. It is important to acknowledge that a chance won't be there for ever. Perhaps it's just a matter of priorities.

You say you've come to a Greek island once. Do you remember which one it was? Although I'm fairly ignorant on other parts of European geography, I reckon that I'm an expert on Greek islands. I've been to most of them. If you ever decide to come to Greece again, I could probably be of use to you.

I've become too talkative again! I hope you haven't got sick and tired of reading this over-long letter.
Affectionately,
Anna

Anna sent the message and switched off the computer. Once more she had forgotten to place that mail order for the poetry books that she wanted.

(Lake District, UK)

The sound of a tractor was all that disturbed the peace of the scene. It was ebbing and flowing as the machine rounded the field on the far side of the garden. Nigel could see that it was chain harrowing the grassy field, no doubt readying it for a batch of young lambs. It was strange how farmers always seemed to be in possession of a first-rate weather forecast. He wondered if the weather would be settled now for at least a couple of days.

Zenca emerged from the French windows with a coffee pot in her hand. "Thought you might like a bit of a top-up?"

"Thanks. Your English is nearly perfect now, you seem to manage our weird colloquialisms like 'top up'."

She poured coffee into his breakfast cup and moved off indoors. Funny lass, he thought, not very communicative, but just what I need though to keep the house going – and to keep an eye on Judith.

Yesterday had been one of the most embarrassing of his wife's 'moments', and certainly the most potentially dangerous. Steve could so easily have been killed, and yet Judith seemed almost totally detached from any sense of responsibility for what she might have done.

He and Judith had married because it had seemed so much the right thing to do. Their families had lived within a few miles of each other in Suffolk and whilst they were not close friends their respective parents were on the same 'dinner circuit' so were rather more than nodding acquaintances. Although he and Judith had met once or twice during their schooldays, they had both been away from home then, so it was not until they both found themselves together in their late teens that they became close. She had been attractive enough to excite a string of would-be boyfriends, and had certainly enjoyed male company, although when they eventually had sex he was a little surprised to discover that she was still a virgin.

He hadn't really intended that they should become a couple, and had not gone out of his way in pursuit of her. Perhaps, he thought, it was that which attracted her to him. Their affair had lasted on and off for a couple of years, before they had drifted apart. He had studied Naval Architecture in London as a three-year course whilst her Media Studies diploma in Exeter had only been for two. She had taken a job in Manchester after that. He had missed her as he liked her very much, but he didn't love her, and for the next four years they had met occasionally at various parties and gatherings. It was following one of the former that they had walked back to her flat, both rather the worse for wear.

They had sex together more as friends than lovers, just two ex-lovers enjoying the end of an evening in close company with each other. Judith had however recently come off the Pill, and Nigel, not aware of that, had failed to use a condom. Neither thought anything of it until some six weeks later Judith had broken the news to him that between the two of them they were about to further expand the human race.

The wedding had been arranged with slightly indecent haste, and had been a grand affair with, it seemed, most of middle class, middle aged, West Suffolk in attendance, leaving little chance for the couple to invite many of their own friends. This had however ensured an extremely expensive and fairly useful collection of wedding presents. Judith had certainly told him that she loved him and, in a formulaic way he had responded in similar vein. Now, he told himself, he had always been unaware of what love really was.

A bit of a commotion inside the house heralded Judith's appearance on the terrace clad in a bathrobe, her drenched hair straggling down the sides of her face. Her feet were bear and there were dark rings around her eyes.

"Don't worry, Mrs Marston, I'll clear it up," Zenca shouted from the hall. Judith looked vaguely at her hands as if expecting an unbroken cup of coffee to re-materialize there. She sat down opposite Nigel.

"Tripped on that damned step again," she explained, "Can't we get something done about it?"

"How are you this morning?" asked Nigel.

"You said you were going to get Tom Dixon to see to it."

"You were in a bit of a state last night. I had to put you to bed."

"I bet you've done nothing about it."

"And you damn near drowned poor Steve, don't you remember?"

"I really can't go on living in this place if you don't get that step fixed; I shall leave."

Zenca appeared with a cup of coffee. She put it down next to Judith and smiled at her, "It's OK, I've got most of the coffee stain out of the carpet."

"Thank you Zenca," said Nigel.

His wife had lapsed into one of her silences. These could last from a few minutes to several hours. Nigel looked at her with a critical eye. She could still have been a presentable woman. Despite the worst efforts of forty-something years, two children, and a great deal of self-indulgence she had retained her slim figure. But her beauty was not now something that radiated from within her, such good looks as she now possessed had, perforce, to be seriously enhanced, if not created, from pots, jars and bottles. She was drinking her coffee slowly and very deliberately, as if a lot depended upon it. Nigel wondered what was going on in that mind of hers.

Judith had never been academically challenged, but she would not have described herself as one of the intelligentsia. She had possessed a cheerful, indeed quite bubbly personality, but if she had indulged in wit it would more often than not have been of a somewhat sarcastic variety, offering barbed comments about others. That said the woman he had married was kind and tolerant enough, and a pleasure to be with. They had lived first of all near Ipswich, and then later moved to the Lake District where they had started the chandlery business. Jimmy had been born six months after the wedding, an event that caused a certain amount of joshing and knowing winks in Nigel's direction from his friends, and then Caroline was born nearly two years later. Caro's birth had not been easy and fairly soon afterwards Judith had a hysterectomy.

"I've made such a bloody mess."

Nigel started. He was surprised that Judith had spoken, albeit softly. 'Don't worry, Zenca's cleared it up."

"No not that, yesterday." Her eyes welled up with tears.

Nigel came over to the white bench seat that Judith was sitting on and put his arm around her. "There was no real harm done, old thing."

"I could have killed him. What's wrong with me, Nige. I just get so carried away. I hardly drank anything"

Nigel's immediate feeling of sympathy was negated by the full knowledge that 'hardly anything' was probably nearer to a couple of bottles of wine.

Whilst he had not been wildly in love with her when they married, they had been through so much together and time and again had relied upon one another. He felt frustrated that he was becoming so intolerant of her and guilty that he always got so cross. Whilst he accepted that alcoholism is a disease, he felt sure that she could do something to help herself – if only she would recognise the problem.

"Look Judy, I am here to help, but I cannot mop up after you forever. You are going to have to do something about the problem yourself."

She rose to her feet and, ignoring his words completely, said. "I'll go and put some clothes on."

Nigel looked at the departing figure of his wife. His left eye was watering. He wiped it. Perhaps it had a piece of grit in it.

He reached for his iPad and checked his mail. Anna had replied, and at some length, and what was more she had reciprocated with a delightful photo of herself. Like his it was passport style just showing head and shoulders, and he had to admit that what he was looking at was a very beautiful woman.

He wondered what he should say to her. It was all very well but he hardly knew the woman, and yet he was more than vaguely aware that he had so much within him that needed to be said. He wondered if he dared confide in her?

> *My Dearest Anna,*
>
> *First of all, many thanks for sending me your photo. I am speechless. You are a very good-looking woman, and to tell you the truth I am just a tiny bit intimidated by that.*
>
> *Of course I am not 'sick and tired' of hearing from you, indeed I feel so happy when I get your e-mails. You write with an openness and a feeling of energy that I really like. Having said that I ought just to mention that the 'net is a dangerous place where people (men and women) entice each other into situations that can accelerate beyond their control. Apparently it is easy to pretend that you are someone quite different from the person that you really are, and in doing so 'groom' the recipient into believing in this fictitious persona. I have a very real trust in you as being exactly the person whom you say that you are.*
>
> *May I speak freely about myself? I was sent away to school from 8 until I was 17 – all boys – and I think this had the effect of making me see women not as proper people, but as objects of desire. After my slightly wild*

early 20's I settled down to try to make a go of marriage, but have to admit that I have made rather a hash of it.

As I explained earlier Judith is far from well although she barely acknowledges this. I am not sure what deep trauma she is trying to expiate, but the outward sign is, I am ashamed to say, drinking. We have tried everything, and so has our local doctor, but J is just unable to control herself. When she has had too much to drink she does stupid and embarrassing things. I have a fear that all will not end well for her although I have tried to be as supportive as I can. I have not spoken so openly about this before, and I find it very difficult to write to you about it, however just at the moment it is such a major factor in my life.

You must so regret not having children. It is wonderful to be able to give them the love and support that they need in life, and to help them grow up into fine and worthwhile human beings. May I ask if it was a conscious decision or a fertility problem? You say that you are a widow. Are you able to tell me how your husband died? Was it recent?

Anna, I hope that I have not overstepped the mark and burdened you with too much intimacy? I seem to have found another human being with whom I can communicate freely and openly, and whilst we could limit our discussions to critiquing poetry I rather think we are already more than a few steps beyond this – and I so welcome your presence in my life, even if it is a 'virtual' one.

With my warmest affection
Nigel x

He worried about that 'X'. Twice he deleted it, only to re-instate it again. What on earth was he up to. An 'X' was only an X, but to him it marked the crossing of a boundary. If she came back to him now, with anything other than the coolest of responses, then they were embarking upon just that which he had warned against at the start of his email, an Internet Relationship.

In any case what was he up to? Just a few moments ago he had been trying to help his wife. Now he was starting out on this man/woman thing with a total stranger. And what about the age difference? It must be at least a decade, possibly more. This really was a case of 'dirty old man' syndrome. He wondered what Caro would say if she knew about it. Probably be very cross with him for being such a stupid, gullible old fool. And yet he had his life to lead. He did not want to hurt Judith needlessly and he certainly felt a strong sense of duty towards her. No doubt the last thing she needed at the moment was a straying husband – even if it was 'virtual straying' and however platonic this relationship with Anna might turn out to be. He noted that he had used the word 'relationship'. He wondered if Anna would be seeing it that way, now that his e-mail was sitting patiently in her in-box waiting to be read.

7

Dearest Nigel,

I was so pleased to see your name glowing in my Inbox. This is the truth, but the content of your message brings with it conflicting thoughts. You discuss so many issues that I really don't know where I should start. I'll give it a try with what you first referred to.

Nigel, your mentioning of the dangers of the Internet has frightened me a little. I have to tell you I'm very new to using it, I only subscribed for a connection earlier this year, and this is the very first time I have had any personal contact with a stranger by this means. (I suppose you'll tell me that this makes me the perfect victim?). When I sent you that first message of support I did not intend, nor imagine that there would be anything more than that. To be honest I did not even expect you to reply. I'm not the kind of person to leap carelessly into any kind of relationship in real life, let alone on the Internet. I am particularly wary because I can't understand if this statement of yours is intended to expresses a warning or is a fear. Perhaps I really should be afraid of you?

And yet, you go on to confess to me all those important, difficult, personal things and in doing so you have touched me in a way that very few people have done for such a long time. I should not say this now, I know, especially after your reminding me of the potential danger, but there is something about you that I cannot resist. For some inexplicable reason I have been drawn close to you, and now feel even closer. I felt this from the very first time I read one of your poems, I don't know why. Even though I've read hundreds of poems on the site - and some might actually be better than yours - you have a way of speaking to a place deep within me. You are inside my heart, or perhaps my subconscious, I am not sure which. But then, if I have not also touched something within you, why would you take the trouble to write to me and to confide in me

I know full well what it means to have experienced traumatic situations, things that are not in your control nor of your choice and yet, to have to endure them and find yourself and your own way through them. I know what if feels like to carry a prickle within, how it hurts, how helpless you might feel about not being able to do something to get rid of it. And though acknowledging that this hurt exists is definitely a kind of progress, sometimes you can't go any further than this acknowledgment, for the wound is so deep within you that you cannot reach down to it.

You will realize that by telling you this, I've also told you a great deal about my soul. But I'm afraid I can't, at the moment, tell you any more detail than this. I'm not ready. It is too raw.

Are you real? I believe time will tell and sooner or later I will know. Am I real? I will have to let you be the judge of that. I have already - yes, quite stupidly - decided to believe that you are who you say you are, if you are prepared to accept that I am who I say I am then, at least for now, we can call this a friendship.

I'll be waiting for your reply.
Very fondly,
Anna

She made a quick check of the message for typos and hit Send without wishing to give herself time for second thoughts. She went back to the Sent folder and read her email again. Blast! Was she out of her mind? Had she gone insane at a moment in her life when there was nobody to advise her? This man was perhaps giving her a chance to forget all about him and save herself from what was potentially a serious situation. He had called their communication a "relationship" although she had not said anything to lead him to the conclusion she was after anything of the sort. She was not.

However, the truth was that his messages, as well as his poetry, exerted an irrational power over her, a kind of attraction she could neither recognise nor wish to categorise. All she knew was that her heart pounded erratically every time she saw his incoming message, and read his words. And the energy she got from them was as if they were from a person she had known for a long time. How stupid could this be, she wondered; probably very stupid; but she admitted to herself that her feelings were also very real.

She had not told him that there was an urge inside her to hug and console him for what he said he had been through. She smiled knowingly at her own self-awareness, knowing that what she was feeling was undoubtedly brought on by her failure to have a child to care for. There could be no doubt that the mothering instinct inside her was craving for emancipation. Given the above she was also sure of her feeling that there was something very strong but equally vulnerable about this man. Might it be this that connected them? She was aware that she was a thing of conflicting emotions; she had been both strong, and equally vulnerable, for the whole of her life. On the other hand, for God's sake, the man was fifty years old! That meant that there was more than 10 years, possibly 12, between them. And yet when she wrote to him or when she read his messages, the impression she received was entirely different from that. It was as if he was very, very close to her in age, in mind, and in distance. Nonsense. She was hallucinating. She should not have isolated herself so completely in this country place of hers. She should not have left all her friends and her circle of acquaintances behind to come and live here on her own. Now she seemed to be so much enveloped in her own loneliness that she found herself ready to trust this absolute stranger. What if he were totally nuts? He had almost admitted that in his message. What if he was one of those stalkers that she would never be able to get rid of, and who would pester her, or worse, forever? The funny thing was, she thought, that she would not have had any of these thoughts had he not warned her against these very dangers.

She remembered that book order that she had meant to place, the one she kept on forgetting. At last she managed to navigate to the book site and completed her purchase. At least she had done something productive, if that could be perceived as such.

Her thoughts returned to Nigel. Why did he have to place so much importance on their innocent communication? Why did he have to go so far with his thoughts about it? She was concerned that she might be stepping over a threshold she did not recognise and that Nigel did. And he was telling her that she was crossing a line. Did she want to cross it? No, Christ, she did not want to cross any line. All she knew was that she wanted to hear from him again.

She spent the rest of the day in trivial occupations. She washed the dishes. She made the bed. She went to the village supermarket. She cooked. She had another cup of coffee. She read a poetry book. She dusted. She mopped. She had lunch late in the afternoon. She pondered on the new job she was about to start very shortly. She wondered what the kids would be like. She wondered if they would like her. She wondered if she would like them.

She went to the bedroom with intention of taking a nap for an hour or so. She didn't sleep a wink. She got out of bed irritated. She had a shower. She put on a nice knitted, woollen, rather short dress. She looked herself in the mirror. Yes. She was still pretty much OK. She turned on the radio. The music was either too depressing or too stupidly cheerful. Irritating in both cases. Abruptly she turned off the radio.

She would have liked to sit outside, in the yard, but now it was too late. It was already dark outside. She put another log on the fire. She decided that it was an acceptable time of day to enjoy some alcohol, so she treated herself to a glass of red wine. Then another. She smoked six cigarettes in a row. She stared at her computer with a look that was nothing short of suspicious. She switched it on. No excuses this time, she had already placed that order for the books. Perhaps she wanted to drop by the poetry site? Oh, how pathetic, she thought. What she wanted to do was check her inbox. She dreaded seeing an incoming message but she dreaded even more not seeing one.

There was nothing; only Nigel's last messages. Last indeed. She read his most recent again; and again; and again. She felt utterly stupid and tired. She went to bed. She slept and dreamed of Panos. He was standing in the distance, sort of mocking her and she shouted at him, she shouted with all her might that he was ridiculous. Panos smiled.

She got up the next morning without much of a plan. She made coffee. She drank it and smoked a couple of cigarettes. She went out in the yard to check if the flowers needed water. They didn't. She thought she ought to get herself a dog. She loved dogs. She hadn't been able to have one in the apartment as Panos had despised animal hair so much.

She looked at her laptop, peacefully resting on the desk. Well, what she liked to call her desk, that wooden kitchen table she had pressed into 'desk service', but after all, she thought, is not reality just what we choose to call it? She hesitantly opened the laptop and switched it on. It seemed to take ages to boot: the windows logo . . . connecting... the blue screen . . . the password request . . . she entered the password . . . connecting... black screen for a while. She feared that it might be infected by some virus. Nonsense. She had the most expensive antivirus software and besides, she didn't really visit any potentially dangerous sites. The main screen appeared at last. She hit the icon that would lead her to the Internet connection button. More waiting. . . and more . . . and more. The signal sucked today. What did she expect at the foot of a mountain two kilometres away from the village? She should consider herself lucky that she had any signal at all.

The icon "Connection" emerged in glory. She hit it impatiently. It opened the main e-mail page. Irrationally her heart was thumping away inside her chest. Her mail provider page covered the whole of her screen. Nigel's last message winked boringly at her. No new mail. With some annoyance she switched off the computer. No 'some annoyance was not the expression she wanted; it was too civilised. She was totally pissed off. And then she scolded herself. What right did she have to feel this way? Come on, the man was probably doing her a favour. She thought of him. He was fifty years old, married, troubled in many ways, and an Englishman. What a joke. She was quite definitely crazy. She wondered what he looked like in reality. Not that she cared at all, but it would at least have been nice to know.

Anna picked up her mobile and selected her parents' number. As usual, her mother answered the phone.

"Mum? Hi, how are you?" she asked with longing in her voice. She missed her parents although her mother called her most days. Sometimes she answered, at other times she did not. Often they would talk for at least an hour, at others she would just find any suitable excuse, an urgent job that she had to do, another incoming call or any other reason she could come up with to say goodbye. She loved her parents, but that initial lie about Panos had set up a barrier in her communication with them. She was constantly afraid that the truth would eventually come out. Something that she would say when relaxed, or perhaps absent-minded, or emotional, would lead to her revealing just a hint of the truth. Maybe an unintended but betraying sentence would fall from her lips and be picked up by her mother's inquisitive, searching nature.

"Hi honey, we're fine. Well, as fine as one can be these days. Your father is really depressed and I am worried about his heart condition despite the pills. He got his pension today, and you can't imagine how little it is now, honestly I'm ashamed to tell you. After all those years of hard work they just say to him that he doesn't warrant the money that he is entitled to. What's more the tax bill arrived by the same post. We don't know how on earth we're going to make ends meet. Oh darling, I'm sorry, I have started off by grumbling and I haven't even asked you how you are doing. By the way, I was calling you yesterday, where have you been? You never answered, nor called me back. Are you ok my little girl? I'm so worried for you. You shouldn't have gone off there all by yourself, you should have come to us, here. Sometimes I wonder, what are you trying to do? You've almost become a nun but without the benefits of life in a monastery!

Why don't you find yourself a nice Greek man? You've mourned for poor Panos long enough, and keeping yourself in such isolation isn't going to bring him back! Anna, you're nearing forty, time passes faster than you realise! After all, if Panos loved you, he would surely have wanted you to be happy!" Her mother took a breath. That was definitely some speech, interlaced as it was with a barrage of questions. Anna found herself in this same uncomfortable position every time her mother brought up the question of her finding another man. She realised that it was an expression of concern, but it was a concern that was being constantly re-cycled.

"I'm fine mum" she said when she could get a word in. Don't worry, everything will find its way in its own time. When you called yesterday I was most probably taking a shower. I didn't even hear the phone ring. I saw the call afterwards, but it was too late to call you back. I've missed you. I'm thinking of driving over to see you before long, perhaps after I have started work. I'm really quite nervous about the job."

"Ok baby, we'll be here, waiting. Come when you feel like it. And you shouldn't worry about the job. You're so talented, and I know you love children, you'll do just fine." Her mother was talking in the most encouraging of tones.

"I know, thanks mum. Talk to you tomorrow."

"Ok baby, take care of yourself. We'll be waiting."

"Give Dad a hug from me."

"Yes baby, I will" her mother replied softly.

Anna hung up. She would definitely go and pay them a visit as soon as possible. They were getting very old now, and Anna was saddened in comparing the current image of her parents with the strong, solid people they had once been. They had both been forceful, in their different ways and according to their own fashion. She wondered how such strong personalities had managed to stay together for so long. Perhaps it was thanks to the fact that they were, after all, so different.

She started her daily round of housework, but cooking seemed way too much trouble today. She feared that if she dealt with it as drudgery the food would come out tasteless. She had noticed that. When she felt tasteless in herself, then no spice, no onion and no garlic was sufficient for her to cook good food. It was as if all the ingredients were absorbed by her dryness, and as if all the subtle flavours simply disappeared into a black hole. She would then have to push herself to eat such tasteless food or be forced to admit that the dish was a complete failure and throw it away. But as the economic situation was now, dumping food was almost a sin.

Anna decided that if she was going to throw money away she might as well do it in a reasonably pleasant manner. She put on a coat and drove to 'Nikola's Blue', the coastal tavern where she had been a few days ago. During a regular weekday as it was today, she was bound to be the only customer there. So much the better, she thought.

She was wrong. There were two old men sitting separately at their respective tables. Both were quietly reading their daily newspapers and sipping what looked like Retsina whilst enjoying a small snack. How odd she thought. They must know each other, Why don't the sit together?

She supposed they were a couple of widowers. She too was a widow, but in coming alone to this taverna she was, as a woman, breaking several village taboos.

First one, and then the other of the men started taking furtive glances at her from behind their papers. They would not speak to her, she was sure of that, but goodness knows what lascivious thoughts were rattling around in their aged heads. She looked boldly at one of them as he furtively eyed her, and raised her eyebrows in encouragement. He hastily looked away. She was being naughty and rather enjoying it. When she got home it was almost dark. She took care of the fire that was drifting into non-existence, and switched on the computer. No message still. She clicked on Compose.

> *Dear Nigel,*
> *It seems that my message has slipped your attention? I'm a bit worried by this silence. Is your wife all right? Are you ok?*
> *If this is a sign you don't wish further contact, I understand. After all you were right. The Internet can be a dangerous place and I'm being so naïve or careless that I seem to have overlooked that. It was a pleasure to get to know you though. I'll keep an eye on the site for your poems.*
> *Take care,*
> *Anna"*

So much for that, she thought, and switched off the computer.

(Lake District, UK)

The blasted lawn mower would not start. This was the first, very early, mow of the season and there did not seem to be any reason for the machine to be behaving so unreasonably. When he had put it away last autumn the engine had been sweet and happy. Now Nigel was faced with a recalcitrant chunk of useless metal. He decided that kicking the beastly thing would do more harm to him than the mower and was unlikely to cure it. Instead he fiddled around with a plug spanner, muttering dark things about all matters mechanical. It was a Hayter mower – and the irony in the name suddenly struck

Nigel and he laughed out loud. Yes, it was a Hayter - and he was a lawn mower hater!

"You laughing or crying Mr Marston?" Zenca had emerged from the scullery door with a plastic basket of washing in her arms, no doubt heading for the clothes line.

"Just venting my frustration on this blasted beast,"

"It won't go if you swear at it. You have to be nice to it."

"Please run, you lovely machine," said Nigel and gave pull-cord a sharp tug. The mower started immediately and ran smoothly in all innocence of any distress that it might have caused. "How do you do it, Zenca. You are my lucky charm." The Polish woman smiled and started to hang out the washing whilst Nigel and his beautifully behaved lawn mower headed for the back lawn.

There is a certain therapy in the mowing of lawns. The buzz of the motor drowns out any distracting sound whilst the repetitive walking back and forth, keeping to the line, means that the eye perceives little else but the very immediate surrounding. Nigel's mind slotted into 'idle'. He thought about this contended life that he was leading. He and Judith were not particularly well off, but they were comfortable enough. His remaining business was bringing in almost enough to live on and in another few years he would get a substantial pension. In the meantime there was no real reason why they should not supplement their income by living off their capital.

He found himself thinking about Anna's country and the mess that ordinary middle-class people were in over there. Pensions, it seemed, were being slashed and for those of working age there must be the constant threat, if not the reality, of redundancy. Bloody mess really. okay in 'legal' terms it could be said to be the fault of the Greek state for not coming clean about their finances when they joined the Euro, but it was not just them Most of the then members of the common currency had been keen to help Greece slide past the formal financial hurdles and thus many a blind eye had been turned. He wondered how it could possibly be in the interest of the vast majority of Greeks to stay in the Euro when to most reasonable observers such a course of action would seem masochistic. For goodness sake he thought, as he negotiated the mower around a flower bed, they would be looking at an austerity programme not just for a couple of years, not even for ten years, but for much of the lifetime of the present population.

The mower started to splutter, he altered the throttle setting, but the damn thing died on him. Annoyed, he marched off to the tool shed and came back with a plug spanner. He looked at the business end of the plug. Nothing wrong here, a nice mid-brownish colour and no trace of surplus fuel. He wondered if there was a problem with the carburettor float. He tramped his way back and returned with a screwdriver, eventually managing to extract the float casing. No fuel flowed out, apart from the little that remained in the bottom of the bowl. The system was bone dry. "Oh Bugger it" he exclaimed, startling a pair of collared doves from the nearby beech tree "The blasted thing is out of fuel." Feeling totally stupid and annoyed with himself he replaced the float assembly, tightened the plug, took his tools back to the shed and returned to the mower with fuel can and funnel. It started on the second pull.

In the midst of this crisis in the grass-cutting arena he had rather lost his train of thought. He returned to thinking about his comfortable existence. He was pleased to have found an emotional outlet in the writing of poetry, although he had not got as much as he had expected out of the poetry writing sessions that he had attended last year. Everyone seemed to applaud Free Verse and whilst he could see its merits in certain circumstances he very much enjoyed the rigours of stanza and rhyme. Sonnets were a favourite of his, preferring the Shakespearian to other forms. He recalled with a sardonic grin how one of his fellow attendees of those writing at The Brewery Arts had suggested that it was perfectly acceptable to modify the syllable count in a couple of lines if that fitted the sense of the piece better. It had horrified Nigel. Sonnets, in his opinion, should be written in Iambic Pentameter, and nothing else would do – that was the fun of it, being able to captivate his creativity within strict limitations. A vague idea flashed through his consciousness that maybe he tended to live his life in such a way – controlled expressionism – now there was a concept for him to conjure with.

He had received a phone call from Lynn early that morning asking if they would both like to come to the surgery and have a bit of a chat with her about Judith's condition. They were good these doctors, there were two of them, a man and a woman, working alternate days, and looking after a small resident population that was engulfed during the summer months by tourists and itinerants in the hospitality trade. There was no booking system for the morning and evening surgeries, you just turned up and took your place. However both doctors were happy to make appointments out of surgery hours and thus it was that Judith and he walked down to the village just before three o'clock.

Lynn herself answered his ring on the outer door of the converted building and ushered them both into her surgery. She was small, flaxen-haired and very vivacious. She was also an excellent GP and Judith liked her, which was an enormous help. Lynn asked Judith to talk through her recent mood swings. This she did and both she and Nigel recounted the embarrassment of the boat trip.

Lynn listened attentively. "What I am about to say may or may not be correct, I just don't know," she said. "Up to now we have been dealing with this problem as one solely related to alcoholism."

Judith half rose to protest, but Lynn waved her down. "Hang on, just hear me out." Judith sat.

"I recently attended a seminar on compulsive disorders and found myself speaking to a colleague who is something of a specialist in such matters. Without of course revealing your identity I had a brief discussion with him about your problem.

"Oh I say," said Nigel. "Was that wise?"

"Well yes, I think so, mainly because he started talking to me about mood swings. He asked if you exhibited such symptoms and I confirmed that. He explained that whilst the primary condition that was exhibiting was indeed alcohol induced there may well be an element of bi-polar involved."

"Is this common," asked Nigel, "and more importantly is there a cure?"

"A large number of people who are bi-polar also have a drinking problem," said Lynn, but it is not so common to see a bi-polar problem arise from alcoholism. And in answer to the second part of your question, I do not want to raise any false hopes of any sort of remission, let alone a cure. However, I would like to carry out some further tests, Judith, and although we have done this before I would like to go through some questions with you."

Judith shrugged. "Whatever." She said.

"Would we eventually qualify for any care assistance?" Asked Nigel.

"Not now. That's all a thing of the past, except for severe cases – and even then there is what amounts to a means test. But you do have some help don't you?"

"Yes," said Judith, "we have a Polish girl, she can hardly boil an egg, but she does the cleaning."

"Ah yes, Zenca," said Lynn, "but she keeps you company when Nigel is out?"

"I don't know why everyone thinks that I need looking after. I am quite capable, really I am."

"All the same, with your condition, I would want you to have someone in the house with you, just in case anything should happen."

'That's usually me," said Nigel, "but Zenca is very flexible about coming over for an evening if I am out."

Lynn said she would be in touch again very soon.

As they left the surgery Judith turned to Nigel, and in a rather loud voice exclaimed, "Bollocks!"

"I thought you liked Lynn?"

I do, but one, I am not an alcoholic, and two I may get a bit tetchy at times, but I am not Manic-Depressive."

Despite the denial of her condition Judith was having one of her better days and as they walked home Nigel was emboldened to suggest that they went out for an early supper combined with a film at Zeffirelli's in Ambleside. A little to his surprise Judith readily agreed to the idea and, whilst he changed back into his gardening clothes, she spent the next hour luxuriating in a foam bath and then thoroughly pampering herself with powder, perfume and moisturizing creams. It was a very sophisticated Judith that floated downstairs to find that Nigel was still wearing a scruffy green top over a well-worn pair of corduroy trousers, his almost totally grey hair tousled and his hands covered in black oil.

"What the hell do you look like? You told me that we were leaving for Zeffs at six o'clock."

"Just make it in time," said Nigel, glancing at his watch that was showing all but six. He stripped off in the bathroom, no time for a shower. He sloshed water over his face and under his armpits, looked at himself in the mirror and applied Judith's clean flannel to a smear of oil on his left cheek, The cheek emerged pink and clean, the flannel not so. Hastily he tried to wash the flannel, failed, slipped into a fresh shirt and a pair of brick red trousers, grabbed his suede jacket from an untidy pile in his cupboard and was on the last step of the staircase just as the long-case clock finished striking six.

Judith put down her empty glass and looked at him coolly. "I do hope we are going to enjoy the evening," she said, and marched out to the car.

Their vegetarian meal was good, and the wine perfect. Nigel enjoyed meat, but was happy to eat really good veggie food – and this was excellent. The meal and film were a 'package' so they were ushered from their table at just the right time to take their seats for the film. Judith however decided she needed to go to for a pee. Nigel and the usherette waited outside the ladies' lavatory. At first they waited patiently. Then they waited impatiently. Finally the girl, concerned that the film was about to start, went into the ladies to find out whether Judith needed any help. She emerged looking ashen faced. "I think you had better come in, sir."

Judith was sitting on the floor, propped up in a corner. Her lovely dress was ripped and floor around her was covered with water, which was, to a limited extent, being absorbed by a morass of toilet paper and paper towelling. Judith was shuddering uncontrollably and tears were streaming down her cheeks, revealing themselves as black lines of mascara.

Nigel and the usherette lifted her to her feet. She was soaked and her torn dress revealed her rather scanty underwear. Nigel took his jacket off and draped it around her shoulders. It more or less preserved the decencies. He fetched the car and Judith, still sobbing, collapsed into the passenger seat. The journey home was silent. Nigel was trying to imagine what had happened in the ladies, but in many ways it did not matter. Whatever it was it had been caused by Judith, and she had been her own victim. For the second time that week Nigel helped his wife upstairs, stripped her tattered dress off her and put her to bed.

He let Tiddles into the house, made sure all the doors and windows were secure, and sat down at his desk, head in his hands. For the first time for many years Nigel started to cry. An hour later he too took himself to bed.

The next morning Judith said she would stay in bed. Nigel brought her some tea and toast. He wondered if she would say anything about yesterday evening, but at present she seemed just preoccupied, living in the moment. He would wait and see.

It was not therefore until nearly ten o'clock that Nigel looked at his e-mails. His heartbeat quickened slightly as he saw that there were two from Anna. He just wanted to imagine that she could give him a big friendly hug and tell him that the world was a loving, caring place. He was surprised to find within him a need for her support and reassurance. He read her first e-mail and felt a glow of pleasure in that she was responding so sensibly and in such a kindly manner. He appreciated that and experienced a warm glow of pleasure upon reading her sentiments.

No sooner had he recognized such a pleasurable reaction as a feeling of warm friendship than it was totally extinguished by the formality of her short second note. Whilst expressing some concern for him, and for Judith, she had flung that bit about 'Internet Relationships' back at him, more or less saying that he had led her on towards some sort of fellow-feeling and then dumped her once she had opened up to him – even if only in a limited way. Bugger it. It was hardly his fault that he had not replied, but he was sorry that things were not working out. He had upset Anna, and suddenly he was very upset with himself

He sat down and pondered. Tiddles came and went. Zenca left him an extremely strong, black espresso.

8 ▌

<u>(Athens, Greece)</u>

It had been a good idea to come to Athens to see Ellie. Anna rarely visited the city these days and whilst she would have hated to live there now, she found the bustle and smell and busyness of the place stimulating.

They were back at their favourite spot for coffee, mulling over their lives, well Anna's life to be more accurate.

She started rather hesitantly, telling Ellie that she was not sure if what she needed in her life could actually be found in a Greek man.

"But you loved Panos, certainly to start with, and he was Greek."

"I was young, he was handsome, he was attentive, he made love beautifully and I trusted him totally, he was so very believable. But look what happened."

"That doesn't mean all our men a tarred with the same brush."

"What I need from a man is intellectual stimulation, followed by emotional empathy. The physical thing is very important, but to me that comes after everything else."

"And just what is this 'everything else'?"

Anna had put herself in a position where she had to tell Ellie about her contact with this older Englishman, Nigel, and how she was starting to feel very close to him and how that was something she found difficult to understand. "All I can say is that my heart pounds erratically every time I see his incoming messages, and read his words."

"This is a fantasy; you have no idea what he's like."

"But it's the energy I get from his words. It's as if they are from a person I've known for a long time."

"Come on, girlie, that's crazy."

"I know, and I'm not happy with myself for being so stupid, but this feeling of mine about him, it's so very real."

Ellie looked worried, very much concerned about Anna. She knew Anna to be a strong character, but equally that for much of her life, particularly in her early years, she had been very vulnerable. "How old is this Nigel?"

She decided it best to shave a year or two off his age to make him seem more acceptable. "He's nearly fifty."

"Oh, for God's sake, he is a good deal older that you are, and how do you know he's telling you the truth? He may be well into his sixties for all you know. What the hell do you think you are doing?"

"When I write to him or read his messages, the feeling I get is oh so different from that. I get the impression that he is very, very near to me. Close in age, in mind, and in distance."

It was a hot day. Ellie waved at the waitress and ordered two Frappé.

She returned to the conversation. "Look, you're hallucinating. You've gone and isolated yourself in that country place of yours. You've left all your friends and acquaintances behind to go and live there entirely on your own. Now you're so enveloped in your own loneliness that you find yourself ready to trust this absolute stranger."

"But he's not a stranger, not to me."

"This is the internet, you fool. He could be anybody. What if he's totally nuts? What if he's one of those stalkers that you can never get rid of, and who would pester you or worse, forever?"

"I know. You're right and I've thought about all that. I know there are dangers out there, but, Ellie, I really trust this man."

"You and your 'thing' about Trust. You trusted Panos, and look where that ended up."

Anna knew that Ellie had a point, she had trusted Panos, and that despite his strange ways. She recalled how he hated the thought of any kind of life at all, other than herself of course, in their apartment. How strange that in his 'other existence' he had been happy to have two children with that Stella.

It was as if he were punishing her for something. She tried to explain this to Ellie.

"I did trust him, but he condemned me to an unsatisfying, deprived, golden incarceration. I have no idea why."

"Perhaps you hurt him in some way?"

"No, I'm sure it wasn't that, at least not consciously."

"Then why? In fact why did you marry him? I know it wasn't love at first sight. I remember how he chased after you for a long time."

"Before I gave in."

"Exactly."

Why had she given in? It had been a long time ago and she was not sure she could remember. Perhaps out of flattery. Perhaps out of boredom, or perhaps because he had managed, in that persistent way of his, to penetrate her defences, to enchant her. And he had indeed done so.

"And then I just surrendered to him. But I never let go of myself completely."

"What do you mean?"

"Panos wanted my total mental subjugation to him, and that I knew I could never give. It was a line in the sand that I believed I would not cross, the allowing of myself to be absorbed, to become just a part of 'we'."

"And when he could not subjugate you he lost interest? He went off in search of a more malleable partner, a different life?"

"Maybe that was it. I never went so far in surrendering my individuality, and because of that I lost him. I realize now that I never became what Panos really wanted"

"And what was it that you would not give him?"

"Oh Ellie, my heart was all his, and my body, indeed almost all of the rest of me. But he was looking for obedience, and it was my soul that rebelled at such a surrender."

(Lake District, UK)

The day had dawned fair, the sun shining as if it knew how much it was needed this day of the annual village festivities. Despite this the very last thing that Nigel wanted to do was to open the village fete. It seemed that following his 'success' at the awards ceremony, he was now regarded as a minor local celebrity, and as such was expected to perform.

He would have been so much happier, on a wonderful day like this, to be walking the fells with his young nephew, Charles. But there was nothing for it but to get up and prepare himself for the event. At least Charles would enjoy it, probably a lot more than he would have liked, especially the fell walking.

This nonsense was due to start at ten thirty so he had time for a leisurely breakfast. Charles turned up on his bike and clattered about getting excited. Nigel told him to go out and run around in the garden until he had finished eating. As he sipped his coffee he watched Charles tearing around the lawn pretending as so many boys have done before him that he is a dive bomber. Nigel knew that his nephew would be going away to school in the near future and realized that he would miss the lad. However there were few boys of his age in the area and it would be good for him to meet new friends.

Zenca came in to clear away the breakfast things. "Are you coming to the fete, Zenca?'

She smiled. "Of course. I love it. It's so traditional."

Yes, the fete was traditional with many of the sideshows dating back to Victorian times. The whole village would be there as well as numerous American tourists exclaiming over the 'authenticity' of it all.

He read Anna's two e-mails, the last with some concern. He could understand that she felt he was neglecting her, and not surprised that she was questioning their newfound friendship.

> *My Dearest Anna,*
>
> *I am so very sorry to have upset you. Friendship starts as a tender plant, needing constant care and nourishment and fostering. I have failed to give it that, and have therefor failed you. The good news is that as it grows such fellow feeling puts down strong, deep roots and thus flourishes and becomes a tough and resilient tree well capable of withstanding the storms and other vicissitudes that life and time hurl at it. I hope that we can develop such a friendship and let it blossom into something greater than that. I*

*am in such need of a friend. That is not to say that I do
not have friends already, I think what I really mean is a
confidante – someone to whom I can express my feelings in
an unrestrained and open way – and that is very difficult
for an Englishman amongst Englishmen for we are by our
very culture not expected to show our emotions. The other
evening, after more problems with Judith, I cried myself
to sleep. You are the first person whom I have ever dared
confess this to.*

*So please forgive me for failing to reply to your kindly
meant and much appreciated earlier email. It would
never have been my intention that I should ignore you. It
is just that I have been away for a couple of days letting my
nephew, Charles, get an idea about the school he is going to
next term.*

*As you will realise I am becoming highly 'addicted' to
your e-mails – they seem, no you seem, to touch a chord
within me that resounds with pleasure. I do hope so very
much that I have not totally put you off corresponding with
me, and that I will hear back from you. I like to think that
we could be the closest of friends, across age and distance
and our own domestic lives. On the other hand I will quite
understand if, upon reading this, you decide that such a
relationship is not for you.*

With much affection,
Nigel x

He had the message written and sent just in time. Charles
and Zenca were waiting for him, the former a trifle impatiently,
in the hall. All three of them walked down together. Nigel
could have brought the car but it was only a short step and

parking in one of the local farm fields was haphazard to say the least. The previous year Nigel had enjoyed himself, spending several hours with the Landrover winching cars out of the rain-sodden fields.

As they walked across the Green Nigel was greeted by several acquaintances some of whom congratulated him on his award. Would he ever rid himself of this millstone? Anyway he had a speech to make and would be glad when it was over.

On the small platform erected in the grounds, Nigel stood between 'Mayoress', this being honorary title only as the village certainly did not warrant a mayor, and the Vicar. He gazed out at the sea of faces and had an uneasy flashback to the last time he had been in a situation such as this. But his speech went down well enough, there was applause, some of which was actually meant, and then it was over. Zenca was with a friend and Charles and he were free to explore the delights of the fete.

It was already quite crowded and people were clustered around the stalls. The pupils from the village school were eagerly pelting their headmaster with water bombs. He grimaced comically at Nigel as he passed and Nigel gave him the thumbs up and made a mental note to buy him a pint in the beer tent once he had dried out. It was decent of the Head to put up with such 'traditional' treatment every year.

Nigel gave Charles some coins and watched him trying in vain to dislodge a coconut. He persuaded Nigel to have a go but he was an even more dismal failure. Nigel suspected that the coconuts were strongly wedged in their holders.

It was very warm so they walked in the direction of the beer tent to buy Charles a lemonade and Nigel a pint of the excellent Hawskhead Bitter, brewed locally, it was a bit of a heady drink for midday, but what the hell, speechmaking time was over. As they approached the tent Nigel could hear raised voices, one of which he recognized with a sinking heart.

Seated at a table inside the tent was Judith. She was drinking with several men who Nigel surmised from their clothes to be Americans. They seemed captivated by her.

"Oh, it's my little Charles," she cried out as they entered. "Come here darling and give your auntie a big hug." Charles reluctantly walked over to her, his head hung low in embarrassment, like a puppy approaching a master who it suspects of being in an uncertain mood.

"There, isn't he a darling?" Judith grabbed hold of her nephew and hugged him tightly to her bosom. The men murmured various compliments. "He's such an absolute darling," she gushed, and I knew that tears were now not far away, these no doubt helped along by several alcoholic beverages consumed over a short period. Most people in the tent were starting to notice her and other conversation had died down.

I ordered my pint and wished I were back home in my den, squirrelled away with my dreams and my loving emails. "And here's my so-called husband, the famous poet," said Judith. There was an edge of sarcasm to her voice and Nigel turned reluctantly to greet the Americans.

"Gee, a real poet?" one man exclaimed, shaking Nigel vigorously by the hand. "Would I have read any of your stuff?"

Judith snorts, loudly. "Stuff is about right. It's absolute rubbish. Bloody silly giving him that award, he certainly never deserved it."

There was a silence and then Judith burst into tears and clutched Charles to her again, "And I'm about to lose this precious boy. That horrible man is allowing his family to send him away to school and he's still just a baby. Poor little boy."

Charles managed to turn his head slightly and eyed Nigel desperately. He was furious. It was hard enough on Charles having to leave home. He wanted to go but he was bound to have some misgivings and this was not helping anyone.

"Abusive, that's what I call it. It should be made illegal," Judith shouted.

Nigel was on a shortening fuse. He pulled Charles away from her. "Well it isn't your decision," he said evenly. "Not that that has ever stopped you interfering before. Come on Charles, we're going."

Nigel placed his hand protectively on Charles' shoulder and they walked out of the tent. People were agog and Nigel's face was hot with embarrassment.

"Don't you walk away from me, you coward," Judith slurred loudly. This was followed by the sound of a table crashing over and of glasses breaking.

The two of them walked quickly through the stalls but the blasted woman came stumbling after them and grabbed hold of Nigel's jacket. He tried to prise her fingers off but she had a strong grip. He pushed her fairly hard and she tumbled backwards, tripping and landing in the plastic pool where the water bombs were being thrown. She staggered to her feet, a pathetic figure now, her straw hat askew and her dress soaked. Several small boys, thinking she was the next volunteer for their treatment, started to pelt her with water bombs. Charles started to giggle and then laugh out loud, that hearty laughter of a boy of his age that comes from the gut. Nigel tried to keep a straight face but really this was such a ridiculous scene.

Judith went quiet as Nigel walked her through the crowds and up to her car. Charles trailed behind them, still convulsed with laughter.

"Give me your keys. I'll drive you home."

She was reluctant at first but even she could just about understand that she was in no fit state to drive. Nigel parked outside the house, opened her door, and unlocked the front door. Judith squelched in and slammed the door behind her. Charles was still grinning broadly.

(Evia, Greece)

Anna was humming to herself, singing the occasional phrase:

> *Eleanor Rigby picks up the rice in the church where a wedding has been*
> *Lives in a dream, Waits at the window wearing a face that she keeps in a jar by the door*
> *Who is it for?*

She took off her pyjamas

> *Father Mackenzie, writing the words to a sermon that no one will hear*
> *No one comes near*
> *Look at him working, darning his socks in the night when there's nobody there*
> *What does he care?*

Moderately warm water came rushing down her body.

> *All the lonely people, where do they all come from?*
> *All the lonely people, where do they all belong?*

She rinsed off the shampoo, then the bath foam, then just indulged in the wonderful sensual feel of the water flowing over her.

> *Eleanor Rigby died in the church and was buried along with her name*
> *Nobody came*

Father Mackenzie, wiping the dirt from his hands as he walks from the grave

No one was saved

She got a freshly ironed towel that smelled of tropical flowers.

All the lonely people, where do they all come from?

All the lonely people, where do they all belong?

She got dressed.

She had been half singing, half murmuring the song for the past thirty minutes. It was turning into a kind of mantra. The Beatles' 'Lonely People' was perhaps the saddest song she had ever heard and she just could not get it out of her head. She had risen just after dawn, taken a shower, put on a formal pair of trousers and a tight, black turtleneck top, and put her hair up in a high ponytail. She continued singing absent-mindedly as she was making her coffee

Today was to be her first day at school and she really wanted to be ready, fully awake and prepared by the time she reached the school gates. What the other teachers would be like? She would be the only stranger there as any other new teachers would have got to know each other by this time of the year. She felt some extra nervousness at this thought.

The ringing of her mobile disrupted her thoughts. It was Ellie.

"Good morning there!" Ellie's voice sounded cheerful but rather sleepy.

"What are you doing awake at this early hour you crazy girl?" She wanted to sound equally cheerful. It was so good to hear from her friend.

"Well, I promised that I'd give you a ring for good luck, didn't I, so here I am, even if it is an unearthly hour of the morning!"

"Yes, you did, but I'd rather expected you to phone me at some more reasonable time, perhaps yesterday, like any normal person might have done."

"I know, but Phillip spent the whole of the evening - and most of the night - here and I sort of forgot myself," Ellie said apologetically. Phillip was now clearly established as Ellie's most recent boyfriend.

"That's all right, you sound like you had a good time, so you're utterly forgiven for not phoning yesterday. Besides, you've just made up for it in the most unexpected way." Anna knew that it must have really cost Ellie to wake up this early. She was most decidedly an owl rather than a lark. They had both laughed at how once, some time ago now, Ellie, the highly professional lawyer, had been reprimanded by a judge and nearly lost her client's case due to her oversleeping and arriving late in court. It was fortunate that she was both talented and clever when she was awake.

"Good luck darling" Ellie said. "Never fear, everything will turn out fine, you've managed far more difficult things than this."

"Thanks" she said, and restrained the wetness that flirted with her eyes. It was so embarrassing getting emotional for no reason. But who was she trying to fool? There was a reason she had become emotional of late, and she hated herself for being so vulnerable.

She picked up her cup of coffee, determined that she wouldn't allow stressful thoughts overwhelm her. To do so would be anything but helpful right now. She looked at her computer. Nigel had answered neither of her emails. The only conclusion that she could draw from that was she should forget all about him. She just hoped he was doing well. Disappearing without a good reason, or without at least some form of farewell did not exactly match her impression of him. But then, what did she really know about him? He had been, and would no doubt always remain, a total stranger to her.

She turned on her laptop, intending to visit the On the Verge of Poetry site. That would relax her and take her mind of the prospect of this anxiety-ridden first day. Those new books she had ordered would be bound to take at least a month before she could hold them in her hands. She always seemed to be waiting for something. Her home page opened revealed Nigel's name, in the bold letters that signified the message to be a new one, cheerfully and hopefully waiting for her in her Inbox. She opened it failing to convince her heartbeat to return to its normal pace. For the tiny seconds before she could read the content of the email, she remained upset not knowing whether the message would bring her joy or disappointment. As her eyes ran line after line, the warm feeling of relief spread within her, making her wonder why this was so important to her. It didn't make sense but she was utterly glad that he had written back, that he was all right, that she meant something to him. She looked at the clock. She had a whole hour ahead of her before she should be getting on her way to that new job. Time enough for a reply.

Dearest Nigel.

I can't possibly tell you how glad I am that I received a reply from you. To be honest, I had been a bit worried about you and could not help wondering if you were all right in health and everything. But I know you so little that I couldn't help the emergence of the doubt that finally resulted in my second email to you.

I'm glad I was wrong in misreading what might be the situation between us, but on the other hand I'm so sorry that you found yourself in such a sad situation that it made you cry. I have an unbearable impulse to ask you what happened to make you do so, but this might seem too intrusive so I just want you to know that if you feel like telling me about it I will be here, interested to listen and more than willing to help in any way I can.

What you tell me about Englishmen and weeping sounds a bit odd to me, I had never realized that this might be part of the culture in your country. In Greece also, men are not supposed to be as expressive as women and this includes crying too, but not as severely, or as strictly as seems to be the case for you. Besides, our culture is changing fast now, and younger Greek men tend to overlook this inhibition, which is now considered more as a hang-up of the older generation. I think it must be really repressing to need to cry and yet not only be unable to do so, but also to be restricted from talking about it! I realise this must be one of the traits woven into the English culture that has led to so many of my countrymen to perceive the English as "cold". Yet it seems that when it really comes to it we all are part of the same dough, sharing the same feelings but just expressing ourselves differently.

Unlike you, I don't have many friends. I'm very diffident about leaping into relationships and, as I've told you before, I left all my circle of acquaintances behind when I left Athens. I still have my one very close friend, a confidant as you say, who lives there. I just wish she lived nearer to me.

I must be on my way now. Today it is the first day of work at school for me. I've been quite nervous about it, but writing to you has helped me relax a bit.

Nigel, I do love receiving your e-mails, and look forward so much to hearing from you again.

Anna x

She put on her jacket, picked up the car keys, looked around in the house in case she had stupidly left something on, but then apart from the cooker that she had used to make her coffee there was no other source of such danger. it was only a short ten-minute drive to the local high school and she put on some music to calm herself. She drove slowly enjoying the scenery, and lowered her window so the fresh morning air softly touched her face. The grass in the fields was vivid and dense, giving the impression of a soft green carpet, inviting her to sit on, or roll on it, and the first wild flowers had made their timid appearance. Daisies for the most part, along with chamomile and some other lighter yellowish ones bearing much smaller bunches of blooms gathered into each stem, and whose name she did not know. Perhaps she could ask somebody at school. She passed a number of almond trees now if full bloom, looking like beautiful earthly clouds with their pink and white flowers.

She liked poppies for their vivid red colour and their fragility, but they would appear much later, April perhaps if the weather was good. they had a way of getting their own back on anyone who took them from mother earth. They withered, not lasting for more than one day at the most, showing how futile it is to think that anyone can actually own beauty. It was surely no coincidence that this flower, gorgeous in its simplicity was also the provider of opium. Daisies on the other hand, did not mind being picked, lasting for days on end just in water and would still smile at the sun, unfolding and stretching out their petals every morning, grateful for what was given to them, deciding to make the most of their lot. She smiled. How closely flowers seemed to resemble the differing attitudes of people.

There was a parking space just outside the High School. Thankfully it was still early enough. She was loath to walk into an office full of strange faces. She got out of the car, stretched her trousers and checked for possible creases, everything seemed fine. She entered the building and paused. She had no idea which way to go for the teacher's office. The place was a labyrinth. Taking pot luck she opened a door. No, that was a classroom. Then another one, but she had no better fortune. She had tried a number of doors when she heard a voice behind her.

"Do you need help?"

It was a middle-aged woman, not very tall with appropriately short black hair done in a style that resembled the way in which her grandmother had hers. The woman smiled politely with an inquiring look.

"Yes" she said "thank you. I'm looking for the teachers' office".

"And you are...?" the sentence remained unfinished, perhaps no one was expecting her?

"Oh I'm sorry, I'm Anna Dimitriou, the new art teacher. I suppose you've been expecting me?"

"Of course dear, pleased to meet you. I'm Helen Vassiliou, the language teacher. I've been here for what it seems like ages and am currently also serving as the deputy head teacher." The woman, maintained her fixed smile which did not exactly radiate warmth. "Come along please, I'll take you to the headmaster's office before I show you to the teachers' room."

Anna followed her to the next floor where it seemed the offices were situated. The woman opened one of several identical doors in a long row. At the far end of the room sat a rather stern man around sixty years old, reading the top paper of a pile of documents on his desk. He turned around as the door opened and bending his head a little he looked at them over his half-moon glasses.

"Mr Konstantinou, this is the surrogate art teacher, Mrs...." The woman seemed to have forgotten her name.

"Anna Dimitriou." She moved forwards to shake the headmaster's hand.

"Hmm," said the headmaster offering her his hand whilst his eyes took in the whole of Anna from top to bottom, in the manner of a living scanner.

"Welcome Mrs Dimitriou, we're happy to have you here," he said somewhat absentmindedly. "Since Mrs. Stavrakou took maternity leave, we have been left without an art teacher so we have been looking forward to your arrival." He spoke in a tone that sounded almost reproachful; as if it were Anna's fault she had not started at the school before now.

"Thank you, Mr. Konstantinou." She would have liked to have added something warmer or more sophisticated, she wanted to make a good first impression on him, but the man had already returned to the perusal of his papers thereby clearly signifying an end to their conversation.

"Come along dear" said the language teacher, "I'll show you to our office".

The teachers' office was packed full. Not with people yet, but desks certainly. It seemed that these had initially been placed in rows but as new staff had been hired, perhaps because the number of students kept growing, extra desks had been wedged into the space between other desks or even in front of them. There really was very little free space left. It reminded Anna of a beehive. There were just seven people in the room as she went in. One woman was making coffee in the little extension room that served as a basic kitchen. A man was reading a newspaper at one of the desks. Two more women were sitting close together in neighbouring desks, leaning towards each other in a discussion that seemed of mutual intense interest but was being conducted in a whisper. Another woman seemed to be trying to sort out a number of sheets of paper that could be students' tests or compositions. A second man, dressed in a tracksuit, was obviously the P.E. teacher. He had his back turned to them and was looking out of the window. The last person, another woman, was just sitting in her desk with a cup of coffee in front of her and seemed to be fighting against falling completely asleep.

As the office door closed behind her and Helen Vassiliou all these people turned towards the new entrants. Since they knew Helen their stares were directed at Anna. Some were gazing at her with curiosity, but the rest noted her almost with indifference. It was only the teacher making coffee in the kitchen who had not realised she was there, or could not be bothered to check her out. Anna took a deep breath to hide the nervousness she was striving not to show.

"Listen up, everybody" said the deputy head teacher loudly "let me introduce you to the new art teacher, Mrs. Anna...." and she paused again.

"Dimitriou" added Anna. This was starting to get on her nerves.

They all smiled at her and the woman who had been in the kitchen poked her head around the door, but no one made a move towards her. Should she go round each of the desks in turn and shake everyone's hand? Instead she just said "Pleased to meet you all" and looked around for a place to sit. She took the first chair she found available, although it was bound belong to another teacher. She could at least occupy it until they arrived. Holding her bag tightly in her lap she looked about her. The faces were still looking at her, smiling at her with what she could only describe as plastic, curious, but scarcely empathetic way. She had not met all the teachers yet, and starts are always difficult. One way or another, she would survive this. She took another deep breath that accidentally ended up as a sigh, but she did not care anymore. Everyone had returned to his or her previous occupation and only the woman who had been battling against falling asleep was still looking at her.

9

There was no response from Anna until the following day. Nigel wondered whether that was due to the time difference between England and Greece. He was not sure whether that was two hours or three hours. There had been times in Nigel's working life when it was essential to know about such matters, now he could not be sure, perhaps it depended upon British Summer Time; the clocks changing at the end of March.

This feeling of hope, almost longing, that came from inside him was a new and rather troubling experience. Would she get back to him? There was something about Anna that touched him deeply, and there was a strong tendency within him to shy away from giving the reason for the existence of this feeling any further consideration.

And now here was reading Anna's latest e-mail. A slight shiver had run through his body when the Mac mail pinged and it was from her. There could be no doubting the effect that any communication from Anna had. Was it because she was so emotionally literate? Perhaps trying to rationalise feelings was not the way to go, better by far just to be swept along with them.

He read the e-mail carefully, and then read it twice more. So, it was clear that she was also totally engaged in their correspondence, and she clearly wanted to know, either out of sympathy or perhaps just curiosity what it was that had troubled him so much. He hoped it was the former, he had a dread of those who live their lives vicariously.

He smiled when he re-read Anna's take on Englishmen and crying. Was that not that exactly what he had been thinking about. He must indeed come across to people like her as being 'cold' and 'unfeeling', but that was just the way he appeared to be. Underneath this bottled-up reserve there was a different, untamed, and passionate Nigel that he was far from sure he wanted to allow out into the daylight. It could well be a genie that would never return to its bottle. And then Anna was telling him that she did not make friends easily. He must have given her the wrong impression about himself. It was easy enough to get on with people at a superficial level, and as such he knew a large number of folk. These were however acquaintances rather than friends. It was not easy to admit that he was bereft of true friends, people, or even a person, that he could confide and trust in. The need had not really arisen, no doubt as a result of his building this impenetrable shield around his innermost thoughts. But now there was a stirring within him, a bubbling of hitherto restrained feelings. It was disturbing. No, it was frightening. But it had him in its grip, this new thing, this desire to share and to be shared. He shivered slightly as he wondered if his wife was right in telling him that he was emotionally inadequate.

He pulled the keyboard towards him and started to write

My very dearest Anna,

He paused. Was this going too far? He felt he had to address her as he felt about her, and after all she had included an 'X' before her name at the end of her last e-mail. He decided to carry on

I am so pleased that you have written back to me in the way that you have. I too feel very much 'at one' with you. I told you that I had many friends, but that is only partially true in that they are really not much more than friendly acquaintances. I have no truly intimate friends at all and was thinking just a few moments ago how totally new it is to me to be able and indeed be keen to confide in you matters that touch the most innermost parts of my personality, things that I have not admitted to anyone else, possibly not even myself

You told me that you have one friend that you can confide in and I just wonder if it might be sensible for you to let her know about me, as a sort of emotional protection for yourself?

Why did I burst into tears? Anna, I had organized a pleasant little evening out because Judith seemed to be doing so well. We had a charming meal together and were off to see a film (The Black Swan). She went to the ladies. I am not sure quite what happened but rather suspect that she had been drinking at home and we certainly shared a bottle of wine with the meal. Perhaps this caught up with her and exaggerated her depressive mood so that she just fell apart when she looked in the mirror whilst trying to smarten herself up a bit. I had to take her home and put her to bed. I accept that this is an illness but it is very difficult to continue caring for her if she refuses to accept her alcoholism. Clearly this manic-depressive thing – bipolar as they now call it - just exaggerates whatever Judith is feeling at the time. So, if she is happy, the world is happy, and if she is sad then we are plunged into melancholy. It is so difficult to keep up with her moods, but I had really thought that she was happy when we left home yesterday evening and that we were going to have a good evening together.

My fear is that I cannot sustain this level of understanding and care for my wife. I am reasonably good at dealing with emergencies – you know, accidents and the like – but it is this relentless and mentally exhausting responsibility that I find so hard. It sounds a terrible thing to admit, but although I am fond of Judith, I am fairly certain I have never loved her. You will despise me for saying such a thing. The only mitigating factor is that for her part she does not, and probably never has, loved me. That does not mean we do not manage together pretty adequately – but hell, Anna, 'adequate' sounds a bit like a life sentence from my new perspective. I am the sort of reserved Englishman who only the vaguest notion of what love really is. Do follow our Royal Family? I don't really, but when Prince Charles was asked if he loved Diana Spencer at a photo shoot when they announced their engagement he said 'Yes,' and then added, sotto voce, "whatever love is." I know exactly how he felt! Was it the Tinman in the Wizard of Oz who was searching for his heart? Perhaps that is what I am doing!

Now tell me about your first day at school (sounds as if I am talking to a 5-year-old!) Is it a good place to be? How were the kids – and the other teachers? Also, you never responded to my earlier question about whether you are happy living on your own. I suppose you might think I am prying, but if we were talking to each other rather than writing from over 1500 miles away then these are the sort of things that would come out naturally in our conversation. The trouble with e-mail is that you cannot see the other person's eyes – and to converse about things that matter that is almost an essential ..

"Nigel where are you?"

He broke off from his writing just as Judith appeared in the doorway of his study.

"I have been looking everywhere for you. Have you been hiding from me?"

Nigel shrugged.

"And who are you writing to? You seem to spend an awful lot of time at that computer these days."

He explained that he was catching up on correspondence with people who were part of the poetry website and that things had got a little out of hand since he had won that prize.

It really would not help matters if he were to mention his e-mail exchanges with Anna, even though there was nothing the least bit improper in them - yet. So why, if the whole exchange was entirely innocent, was he not telling his wife about it? The answer was blindingly obvious but it was one that he really did not want to admit. The word was 'yet', nothing improper 'yet'. Bloody Hell, what was he getting himself into? Was this an innocent correspondence between two creative people, or was it something a great deal more serious – his heart leaped at the answer, amidst a rising sense of shame, shame at the way he was treating his wife, shame at behaving like a classic 'dirty old man' and exploiting a vulnerable woman on the internet. But shame was not the paramount emotion even though he recoiled from naming it.

"Well don't be too long, you promised to take me into Ambleside later for my church meeting." Judith left him to it, and Nigel returned, slightly shaken by his own inner revelations, to his writing. He had rather lost his train of thought so continued with a new paragraph

> *Anna, I know next to nothing about your culture even though I took Classical Greek at school, but that hardly qualifies. I also know next to nothing about you, and I have no idea as to whether you know much about Britain, or have ever been here.*
>
> *We seem to be an oddly matched pair of people. I find this affinity between us incredibly stimulating. I am so keen that this friendship of ours should be allowed to continue and to blossom, I see it as something very precious and very rare, and all the more so because we have never met each other and have such different backgrounds.*
>
> *With the very kindest wishes*
> *Nigel xx*

Unusually for him Nigel read his e-mail very carefully. He corrected a few typos, mainly caused by an over-enthusiastic spell checker. He wondered if he had gone too far. Had he exposed himself too much to this distant and largely unknown Anna? In fact what the hell was he doing writing to her at all? Yet inside him he felt a need. It was like hunger but not so easy to define.

With a surprising degree of self-realisation he understood that he was a lonely man, indeed he lived in a country of lonely men insofar as the English upper-middle classes were concerned, and yet he had recently achieved the milestone of his half century without ever before appreciating that this was his problem.

There was no resentment at having being sent away to boarding school at an early age. Indeed, after the first few 'settling in' days the experience was thoroughly enjoyable. It had been a cosseted existence, that environment of the all-boys prep school set in a magnificent house in delightful parkland with the grounds running down to a navigable estuary. Followed at the age of thirteen by a school some 150 miles from home, again all-boys and again much enjoyed. So, he had emerged well-schooled but poorly educated into the vibrancy of real life and with very little idea about any emotion that did not involve a bat and a ball. No wonder there was a whole cohort of men who, like him, were so separated from their emotional selves that they found it hard to communicate at a deep level with any other human being.

Perhaps this was his 'last chance'. It could be his emotional swan song. He had once read that it was impossible for there to be a truly platonic friendship between a man and a woman, that sex or love or both would always barge in. Well, he intended to prove that this was not the case. Anna lived far away and it was extremely unlikely that they would ever meet, so Plato would be proud of them. With a slight smile he clicked the mouse and an exposition of his fears, and his dreams winged its way to the far end of the Mediterranean at a speed that would have totally flabbergasted the aforementioned Mr Plato and his contemporaries.

The most tremendous rush of relief accompanied this action. It seemed that a burden of many years was lifting from his shoulders, and he struggled to reason why. After all Anna might well be so astonished and upset by his musings, and his requests, that she would close down this 'relationship' before it had gained any legs. So be it. He had tried to find an outlet for his psyche. No harm would have been done if he failed. It was common knowledge that several of his friends (acquaintances?) had affairs with other friend's wives. This was tantamount to 'pissing on your own doorstep' in such a small community. Well if he was guilty of 'emotional pissing' it could hardly be argued that it was on his own doorstep!

With a lighter heart he went in search of his wife, finding her sitting in the conservatory. "You ready for Ambleside now?"

"Oh, Nige," she said, "I really can't face it today."

Normally he might have felt a twinge of exasperation, but such was his mood that he was happy to phone the Church group for her and pass on her apologies. "Come on, old thing," he said, "how about we go out for a bit of a wander instead?"

"I'm not sure, I really don't want to risk meeting anyone."

He took her by the arm and walked out through the glass doors into the garden. The warm early spring sunshine that had played with the snowdrops was now starting to pull the daffodil shoots from their bulbs. The beech hedge was busy shedding its withered reminders of last year and he could hardly wait until it started to bud, unfurling those wonderful, soft lime-coloured leaves that were so susceptible to a late frost. They walked arm in arm around the edge of the lawn, an old couple looking as if they were posing for a Saga advertisement.

They did not say much to each other except to comment on a particular piece of planting, or the need for some edging, or the state of the wooden fence between their garden and the adjoining field. They did not need to.

(Evia, Greece)

-

Anna returned the stare of the woman sitting on the other side of the desk. She was about her age; forty-six at the most, with fair hair, a rather pale face and equally pale blue eyes. For a few moments she seemed to study Anna, then with a natural hesitancy she left her desk and approached her.

"I'm Christina," she said simply, offering her hand. Anna stood up hurriedly to return the handshake whilst with the other hand she grabbed her bag that was slipping from her lap.

"Come, I'll show you around."

Anna followed her outside the office, and along several long corridors from which identical doors lead to identical classrooms, row after row of them, placed one next to the other.

"Thank you" she said as she strived to keep pace with Christina, who seemed to be fully awake now.

"You're welcome, honestly it's no great trouble. I would have liked somebody to have done the same thing for me when I first arrived here. Which school were you at before this?"

"Oh, none. This is my experience with teaching,"

Christina turned to look at her, clearly most surprised. Anna was not exactly young to be starting out on a teaching career.

"I've just moved here a few months ago. I lived in Athens where I made a living as an artist," there was a compulsion to explain herself but a reticence as well, some things were best not spoken of.

"And what made you leave such an interesting profession to come teach here?" Christina seemed to regret asking this question as soon as she had asked it. She hurriedly added "Oh dear, that's rather indiscreet of me, I didn't mean to be nosy, I'm sorry. After all, everybody has their own reasons for doing what they do. But I suppose this is a hard time for selling artwork?"

"Yes, it is indeed. The market has almost totally disappeared"

"I teach religion. Another joke of a lesson here, but I have to say that in some ways I'm in a better position than you." although Christina was smiling that did little to dispel the disquiet that was rising in Anna.

"What do you mean?" she asked in a fog of worry and suspicion.

"Oh, you'll see in time, but I'm afraid I'm making you rather nervous, I'm sorry. Let's take it from the start. This is the ground floor of course; here we mainly have classrooms for the first-year students. As classes go higher, the classrooms also climb up the floors of the building. I believe you've already met out headmaster in his office on the second floor?"

"Yes, I have" said Anna, thinking of the question she had wanted to ask for some time, "Christina, forgive me, I am totally inexperienced as I've told you, but I'm a bit at a loss as what I am expected to do. So far I've not been given any direction. Is there a curriculum to follow? And I wonder if you could possibly show me to the art room?"

"Oh dear, of course there is a curriculum, I'll make sure you get it soon as we return in the office. I'm afraid you've been living on another planet though. There is no art classroom anywhere in the school; you must wonder what you have come to. I can take you to the storeroom where, along with a million other things, we keep the art equipment, but please, for your own sake, do not raise your expectations. Wait a minute, I'll go fetch the key." Said Christina, and sped back to the teachers' office. Anna stood waiting for her in the corridor while noisy, sleepy, cheerful and sullen teenagers passed her by on their way to their classrooms, there to leave their school bags and return quickly to the yard.

Christina was back really soon. She held a big bunch of keys that were jingling as she walked swiftly along the corridor "Come on, we must hurry, the bell will be ringing almost any minute," she said as she turned to the left and hurried along yet another corridor. They were now at the back of the building and here it was much darker. She found the key for the door they were standing at, opened it and fumbled for the light. The room, lacking any windows, was pitch dark. The smell of stale air and of things that were possibly rotting were the first impressions that struck Anna. She slowly became used to the dim electric light. Looking around she could see broken desks untidily heaped in a corner, old green boards, a number of books bound in piles, which seemed to have been there for ages and bearing obvious signs of mould, and big cartons or boxes whose contents were totally obscure. She looked questioningly at Christina. All she could see that was even distantly related to art was a broken easel.

"Well, that's it," said Christina anticipating her question. "You can, of course, bring your own stuff, if you have any, and if you are willing to take the risk for its safety as there would be no guarantee of such."

"And how on earth am I supposed to give an art lesson without any art equipment?" It was a logical enough question. "Do the students themselves have anything that might be related to art or helpful for the lesson?"

"Such as?"

"I don't know, anything. If not oil paints, which I gather would be too much too much to ask for under these circumstances, then perhaps watercolours or pastels or... I don't know, anything one could use for painting?" She sounded quite helpless.

"I can't be sure, but honestly, I think it's very unlikely. You see, this year the students have not even got all the books for their curriculum yet. We're trying to manage with photocopies - and a lot of imagination – well, some of us are."

"What about those piles of books and things over there?" asked Anna.

"Those are just old editions, useless now, and nobody seems to even think about recycling them. Look, don't get too upset, this is your first day. Just get into the classroom, say hello, get to know the students' names if you want, and that should be enough. I'll make a photocopy for you of the curriculum for your lessons, then if you want to you can take it home and have a good look at it". And with that she switched off the light and locked the door, just as he shrilling sound of the school bell was heard.

Anna entered the classroom with her legs shaking. She closed the door behind her and put her bag on the desk. She faced the classroom. All the students were at their desks now, but none of them seemed to be taking any notice of her. They talked very loudly with some of them really yelling to each other, laughing and doing all sorts of things, apart from looking at her. Anna thought she should give them a little time to register her presence and calm down. After several minutes, no such thing happened. She cleared her throat and, in an effort to be heard above the students' voices, shouted at them as loudly as they were shouting.

"Hello, everybody! I'm your new art teacher! My name is Anna Dimitriou." The result was further noise and almost complete chaos. Many of the students just ignored her and continued with what they were doing. "Helloooo!" she shouted even louder, feeling that if she was forced to go on like this she might not be able to speak the next day. That had some effect because some of the students turned around to face her with surprised expressions. Anna was not sure whether they had just noticed that she was there, or if this was a result of her having had the nerve to shout at them like that. "My name's Anna, we will be doing an art lesson together." The sentence was too long, she had already lost some of her audience.

"Art in what sense?" The question came from one of the back rows. Anna stepped to the side so she could see to whom this voice belonged. She identified a curly haired girl who looked at her intensely and smiled faintly, if a bit ironically, as she waited for an answer. Then, as Anna strove for an answer and cleared her throat so she could be heard, the classroom dropped dead silent, waiting to see how she would answer the girl's question. "What is your name dear?"

"Sophia" said the girl confidently, not abandoning her smile.

"Well, look Sophia, I have only just got to know about the situation concerning the art equipment so I suppose your question is more than reasonable What I can tell you is that I will do my best to find some way so that we can get ourselves in touch with art in the best...." She realised that it would be futile to continue talking. Everybody, including Sophia, had resumed their previous occupation, but at an increased volume

She sat down at her desk and just watched them for the rest of the hour until, with the greatest of relief, she heard the sound of the bell.

She arrived at the next classroom with greatly reduced expectations. Same picture, same noise, same pointed neglect. She made a feeble attempt to introduce herself, which, as she expected, was to no avail. She passed the rest of the hour staring at the students, trying to repress her greatest desire, which was to take to her heels and get out of the place as fast as she could. The bell she had once so despised sounded again, and this time it seemed to her to be as pleasing as the beautiful twittering of birds.

She had only one more hour's lesson left that day and she had to exert all her self-discipline to nerve herself to enter the classroom. She took her seat at the desk without a single word. This was a class of younger children, in their first year of high school. Surprisingly, after some five minutes had elapsed with Anna having made no attempt to speak to them, the class started to stare at her, seemingly perplexed. Anna kept looking at them and the children now began to appear slightly nervous. Then, speaking with a clear voice, she started to talk to them, beginning by introducing herself. She continued by asking the children for their names and, against all the odds, she managed to achieve a small degree of rapport with them. The bell came as her saviour again, but this time at least, she had managed to communicate with her class in a simple but effective way.

She almost ran out of the schoolyard. She reached her car, but as she was putting the key in the lock she remembered that she had asked Christina to make a photocopy of the curriculum for her and it would seem impolite at the least, rude at the worst, if she did not drop in to get it. Also, she wanted to thank Christina for all her help she had been in volunteering to assist her, something none of the others seemed to be the least interested or willing to involve themselves in, not even the deputy head teacher Unwillingly, she turned back into the school.

Christina was not in the office, she must have been still taking a class, but she had left the photocopy for her. Anna took it and rushed to the car. The sooner she got out of here, she thought, the better it would be. She had a splitting headache and a feeling of desperate failure. When she had considered the prospect of teaching, apart from the financial side which was now vital to her, she had hoped that she might be able to transmit a little knowledge, a little love for art and a little of its magic. She had indeed, as Christina had put it, been living on another planet. She switched on the engine and accelerated away in a manner that would not have disgraced a racing driver.

At home Anna tossed the pack of photocopies onto the coffee table with rising indignation. Reading this bunch of useless stuff was the last thing she wanted to do. She changed her clothes, ate a light lunch and switched her computer on. It was too early to hope that Nigel might have replied but she couldn't resist the temptation of checking to find out. She was rewarded for so doing. She could not lie to herself about how pleased she was, for although in the past he had taken a day or two to reply to her, now he had sent this on the very same day. This, and definitely the content of his message, signified a kind of progress, although she did not know what they were progressing towards. She wrote.

Dearest Nigel,

It is kind of amazing how your distant contact achieves such a soothing effect upon me. I got into the house a while ago, with my head about to explode and my mood swimming in black waters. And yet, I am now in a position to write to you, feeling so much calmer, as if your words have swept my misfortunes away.

You may well have correctly guessed that I have had one hell of a day. I really can't imagine if it could possibly have been any worse. To cut a long story short, my first day was a total disaster. The teachers I met, all save one, were the most inhospitable or indifferent people I have ever come across. The students were terrible, apathetic and disrespectful beyond imagination. Oh, perhaps I'm being unfair to them. Truth is, these children are asked to attend an art class when there's not one single piece of art equipment in the whole school. And although I'm totally inexperienced both with teaching and with children in general, I can well understand that theirs would be the healthy reaction of any sensible human being upon being expected to endure such absurdity. Actually, it is the word hypocrisy that comes to my mind but I won't take it any further, it has tired me more than enough already.

You ask me if you can confide in me, and you call this a big "ask". But, my dear, this is the best news I've had today. Nigel, I don't know what you think, of me, but I do care for what happens to you, I do care for your messages, which I have to confess I look forward to with more and more anticipation. For a reason I cannot really explain, your emails are important to me. In the light of this, do you think I would be interested in talking about the weather? On the contrary, I can only feel honoured that, of all people, you have chosen me, a total stranger after all, to confide in things that, as you say, you have never felt able to tell anyone else. But I can't restrain myself from asking why.

Again, so sorry to hear about your wife's condition, it must be very hurtful for both of you. As I read about it, the word "trapped" kept coming to my mind, I don't know why, and I'm not even sure you feel this way. And yet, certain things you say indicate to me that you do. I am not on good terms with traps any more. I will do anything to avoid such a situation again. But this is too easy to say when on the outside.

You don't make me dislike you when you reveal the weak sides of yourself. It's only through our weaknesses and faults that we can understand and empathise with each other.. I hope the Tin Man can find his heart, for deep down he too knows that it's only honest emotions that can turn life from a futile waste of time into a real, worthwhile, everlasting experience.

Very Fondly,
Anna x

10

(Lake District, UK)

The conservatory was warming to the attentions of the sun as Nigel replaced the receiver on its cradle. Great, it would be lovely to see Caroline. She would be on her way to a big meeting with some corporate clients in Manchester and thought she would drive on up so that she could drop in and see 'The Crumblies'. She could only manage one night, but it would be wonderful to catch up with her. Where was Judith? She would welcome such news. Wandering into the kitchen he found Zenca instead.

"Have you seen Judith, Zenca?"

"I think Mrs. Marston is in the den, at least she was ten minutes ago."

"OK, thanks. Oh, and could you possibly make the bed up in the middle spare room, Caroline is arriving this evening."

"Will she be staying long?"

"Oh no, she said just the one night, I daresay she will on her way in the morning."

Judith was sitting at his desk. amidst the piles of books and press cuttings that seemed determined to take up permanent residence on his workspace. He was mildly surprised to see her in the room, a few years ago Judith had made use of a table here for minor admin tasks, but for the past couple of years that had become yet another repository for his books. "That was Caro on the phone."

"You bastard."

"Hey, steady on, what's the matter?"

"You cheating, lying horny old bugger."

The conversation did not seem to be flowing along on entirely conventional lines. Nigel made one more, futile, attempt to alert his wife to their daughter's imminent arrival before he moved round behind her as she sat at his desk so that he could see why she was staring fixedly at the computer screen. The Mac Mail application was open displaying the latest email from Anna.

"Why are you reading my mail?" he blurted out, before realizing that this was just like waving a red rag at his spousal bull.

Judith turned on him, her face a picture of the wife scorned. She pointed at some of Anna's innocent words. "Why does this tart say she is worried about you? What is this that you have told her about English people blubbing? Why does she expect you to write back soon – and have you written back to her?"

"Come away, dear, come on, it really is nothing to get upset about."

"Not get upset? This tart is getting you to mentally expose your-self to her. Look at this bit here about there being a deep under-standing between the two of you. What the hell are you up to, and who the blazes is she?"

Nigel very firmly eased Judith from the chair by her left arm and half walked, half pushed, her out of the den into the sitting room. He sat her down on the cream sofa and positioned himself next to her, thus avoiding having to look directly at her.

It's OK," he said. "There's nothing sinister at all about that e-mail. I have been writing to a really pleasant woman in Greece who is a member of the 'On the Verge of Poetry' web group. We have been exploring together some ideas about poetry, as she is interested in us working together so that we can build up sufficient material for a website, and possibly later to publish a small poetry book together. You just got the wrong end of the stick."

Judith was shaking, either from shock or rage, or both. She seemed now to be on the point of bursting into tears. "You are lying to me," she said, "I know she's a tart. She is behaving like a tart. No woman would write like that unless she had designs on you. She wants to take you away from me."

"That really isn't true. Certainly, we are exploring emotions and relationships, but that doesn't make the Anna 'a tart' as you put it. She seems to be a decent, honest, caring person. Yes, I enjoy corresponding with her, but there is nothing improper going on, you've got to believe me. Honestly I think you've got to calm yourself down a bit."

There really was no reason why he should not tell her about Anna, it was not as if it was, or ever could be, anything more than a conversation on the internet between two rather lonely adults. However he recognized with a degree of surprise that he felt quite possessive about this 'relationship'. He did not want to share his involvement with Anna with anyone, least of all his wife,

"What about the tart?" Clearly an element of suspicion still remained.

"You cannot go around calling every woman I speak to a tart or a floosie. You were quite awful with that reporter the other day and now you are being terribly unfair to poor Anna, who has never done you any harm. She lives in Evia, which is a large island north of Athens. About a two hour drive I should think"

Judith seemed just a little mollified by this and nodded her head miserably. She cheered up even more upon learning that Caroline had just been on the phone and that she was coming for supper that evening. However when she realized that her daughter was only coming for one evening she sunk back into depression So it was well over an hour later, following pills, soothing cups of tea and much help from Zenca, that Nigel was able to slip away from a now sleeping Judith and bring up Anna's latest message on his Mac. He read it with much care and a real sense of tenderness. What a very fortunate thing it had been that Judith had not read this message. It was, he tried to convince himself, nothing more than a note between friends, but there was an undercurrent of so much more. He and Anna had already achieved a very special sort of emotional rapport that was hard to define and even harder to explain.

He wondered if he should put some sort of security in place so that Judith could not read his e-mails, well at least not those from Anna. But then if he did so he would be admitting to being involved in something deceptive, something clandestine, something that he did not dare bring into the light of day. That was not how wanted his relationship – yes that word was firmly entrenched now – with Anna to be. This was an experience that he was so fortunate to be enjoying and he was damned if he was going to cheapen it by behaving in a furtive and underhand manner.

He was unsure about how he should reply to this latest e-mail. Rather than think it through too carefully it would surely be better to just let it flow – just like his poetry, it could always be revised later.

> *My very dearest Anna,*
>
> *I find such joy, such exhilaration when I see your e-mail address lying there waiting to be opened. There is such a 'tingle factor' between us. I know you feel it, you have said so, and I most certainly do. I am not just saying this to you because you have provided such a heartfelt and kind response to mine of yesterday, but because that is the way I*

react to your 'presence' – even if that presence is so far away. Why should we both feel like this? For my part, I suppose I must be starved of emotional togetherness, a sharing kind of friendship that has no need to impress or show off in any way.

To discover that I am able to 'open up' to another human being is a wonderful thing, although I have no idea what weird kind of chemistry has enabled this to happen to me. Perhaps I am just a - very – late developer.

I find that writing poetry puts me in touch with a part of myself that I have had to keep battened down for most of my life. Much of my effort and energy had to be channeled into practical, mundane things such as stock control and paying staff, and advising on how to repair a boat. I enjoy practical things and like working with my hands, but there is so much more to existence that just that.

Poetry is a way of expressing things that cannot be easily said as a matter of conversation, even a conversation between friends, and this, I think, is where our 'relationship' is (for we do have a relationship do we not?). I want to be able to confide in you as if I were constructing a poem. It involves ideas, thoughts, emotions - both bidden and unbidden - rising up through my layers of repression and finding expression in my words. And those are the words that I am having the temerity to ask you to receive.

I know you do not want to tell me much about your personal circumstances, and I do of course respect that (although I am here if you do wish to confide in someone).

Wherever this relationship is taking us I have to say that I am enjoying the journey, so I am now looking forward eagerly to hearing from you very soon

With very closest and fondest wishes
Nigel xx

As the message disappeared into the ether he smiled gently at how 'forward' he had been with Anna, wondering what she would make of his words.

(Evia, Greece)

"Good morning, Anna" said Christina in a welcoming way and with a faint smile. Anna had arrived at school early that morning in hope that she would get a moment with Christina before starting her classes. At this hour, there were just the two of them in the office.

"Thank you so much for all the trouble you took in helping me yesterday and for the photocopies of course."

"Not at all. Did you have a chance to look through them?"

"Just a very quick look, but oh it's all so futile! I'll never be able to give these children a real art lesson. The troubling thing is that they knew the situation long before I realised it. You know, I had such a hell of a day yesterday." She was getting disheartened by the thought of another such day.

"Yes, I can imagine, but there's nothing you can do really. In time, and as the children get to know you, things might get a bit better. But even if they don't you'll find that you get used to it." Christina's smile hovered between uncertainly, bitterness, and encouragement, settling on the last.

Surely it was not possible to become anaesthetised to that feeling of contempt from the Authorities; not just towards her as a teacher, but towards the students too. There was also the dreadful realization that the whole system of was collapsing throughout the country, being stifled by the shambles that was now the Greek economic nightmare.

"Did you hear that there will be a strike again tomorrow?" Christina asked, changing in her tone.

"No, I hadn't. Most of the time I'm only barely up to date with the news" said Anna feeling a flush of embarrassment.

Christina looked surprised, but didn't comment on her ignorance. "Perhaps you've heard that they are cutting down on our salaries once again? With this new reduction we'll be lucky if we end up with as much as half of what were paid just a few years back. I am afraid that it is bound to be worse for you of course, as you are a new teacher."

Anna thought about it. She had started with half a pension from Panos, which had already been cut down to fifty percent of the original amount. So she had taken this job to fill in for the missing income, but now this had been reduced by half as well, so it seemed that no matter what she did, she would never, even at best, make more than a pittance. Poverty seemed to be chasing her like her shadow.

"So, will you take part to the strike tomorrow?" asked Christina disrupting Anna's gloomy thoughts. Privately she doubted if this strike, along with all the previous ones, would result in anything more than losing another day of pay. But then again, this was the only "voice" that people like her could bring to the situation, even if government seemed to suffer from extreme deafness and could not hear it.

"If you're asking me if I'm coming to work tomorrow, then no I won't, although, to be honest, I don't see who will be hurt by my absence, except perhaps me. As I see it any strike such as this will only serve to relieve the public finances from having to fund some of our wages, but if that's what you'll be doing I certainly won't spoil it." The one thing she was quite clear about was that she did not wish to lose Christina's newly acquired friendship.

But Christina seemed to understand. "That's my concern too, but do you see any other option?"

No, Anna did not. Indeed, she could not see any really worthwhile options at all. She would have liked to ask Christina what the rest of the teachers thought but just as she was about to do so the deputy head teacher joined them, discouraging her from any such attempt.

"Good morning, ladies" said Helen Vassiliou, wearing a frozenly sweet smile. Then, addressing Anna "Oh I see you've made an early start today dear." And before Anna had managed any sort of response, "So, are you getting accustomed to finding your way around?"

"Well I am far from sure yet," said Anna. "But I really could do with a word with you about something.... as I expect you know, there's not really any available material to carry out my lesson. I'm aware that there's not really much you can do about that, so I was just wondering, is there a projector that can be connected to a computer, so I could at least show some paintings to my students and use this as something that might provide at least some stimulation and interest?"

The false cheerfulness exuded by Mrs. Vassiliou deserted her. She adopted a much more formal tone as she replied, "It's not really my responsibility to consider this, I'll have to talk to the Principal. But, as far as I know, such computers as might be available are all used for the IT lesson, which takes place at the same time as yours, and as this would of course take precedence it would make such an idea quite impossible."

Any last vestige of remaining hope vanished, evaporating from Anna as fast as the frozen smile on Mrs. Vassiliou's thin lips.

"Look dear" Mrs. Vassiliou said, "this is an awkward situation for all of us, these difficult times call for a tightening of all our belts. We'll have to make do with what we have and make the most of it." She spoke firmly and as coldly as ever. Anna had got her answer as to what at least one of the teachers thought about the current situation, but she wondered what on earth it was that she was supposed to 'make the most of'.

"Haven't you had any coffee yet?" Mrs. Vassiliou voice had reverted to the cold cheerfulness that Anna was starting to get used to.

So that would be her lot. She would step into one more classroom, to face yet another bunch of new faces, yet another new class of students. She would greet them and try to introduce herself only to be faced with more scorn. It was only her second day in this place, and she already felt utterly consumed by the system. It was as if she had lost the last morsel of creative spark left within her. All she had to do was to introduce herself – for a whole academic hour! She dreaded the thought of the upcoming week, when she would have finished with introductions, and with excuses. Then she would have to look at those enquiring eyes with both she and her students knowing that they were fooling each other. She would have to talk to them about impressionism and expressionism, cubism and romanticism without a single example of what she was talking about, without the magic or the beauty of those paintings and without a single reason as to why her students might need all this unfruitful knowledge to help them in their lives.

Yet both Christina and Mrs. Vassiliou had been right. She walked into the classrooms on that second day, with all the awareness she had gained, with her legs trembling less, with less anxiety, with less expectation, and with less creative illusion. She knew the trick now. She would remain silent. She would gaze at them. They would get puzzled. She would then proceed to introduce herself. And that would be all. How easy it was indeed to study peoples' behaviour, their responses, their reactions, and manipulate them accordingly. It took but just a little knowledge, just a little interest, just a little skill and there you were. Her interest and her concern, no matter of how little use in the end, were genuine and of good purpose, but she realised that it could have very well been otherwise.

She finished that second day with the same amount of emotional exhaustion but with only a mild headache; the same amount of despair but less involvement; the same care but more self-protection. She would eventually and inevitably get anaesthetised to a certain extent. These teachers were right, they had been there, they knew how to manage. She flopped into her car and accelerated away less abruptly this time, for she knew that a speeding car would not save her from what she wanted to run away from. She also knew that eventually she would cease running away altogether. She would compromise, or pretend that she had done so. In this manner she would be able to survive.

She arrived back at her house with the same feeling of relief that every fugitive must have felt when attaining refuge. She was in her own private world again and everything else could stay outside, wait, until she would have to face it. It was such a relief that she would not have to go to school tomorrow, no matter how much that would cost in material reward.

> *Dearest Nigel,*
> *Your reply takes me into deeper waters in many aspects. As an artist, I have always found deep water much more interesting than shallow, so I will not shy away from it. Why do I really wait for your messages in intense anticipation? Why does my heart lose beats or run so much faster, when I see your name on my screen?*

Why do I relish every single word of your messages, no matter if you're writing about your feelings, your wife, or just the weather? Why during the of the whole day yesterday, when I was dutifully entangled in my misery, did I suddenly got an odd tickling feeling within, something urging me on, so that my thoughts stayed with you for a considerable while. And then, when I came home, I found that this was around the time you had emailed your reply? I don't know. Neither do I understand where this feeling of kinship that I have felt right from our first messages, comes from.

So, are you real, or just a construct of either my own or your imagination? There is only one way I can find out. And this is to trust you. After all, if all that you write to me, if all this bearing of the soul is nothing but the imagined thoughts of a fictional character, you must suffer much more that I will ever do. And yes, I think it is worth the finding out.

Nigel, I don't know what to write to you about the situation with your wife. You say you are not courageous, but in your admitting your qualms and weaknesses and in your resolution to persist with your support despite those, I can only see courage. But I'm not able to tell you whether this will account for a plus in your life's balance book or a minus. I understand it's a kind of sacrifice. But only you can decide whether this is what you really want, whether it is indeed your most important priority. Everything has its own price, nothing we gain in this life is for free.

I have been putting of telling you about what you once described as my 'demons'. You have been so open with me that I feel ashamed not to have let you at least peek into my darkness. I had what I would have called a good marriage. I loved my husband and think that he loved me. There were signs that perhaps I should have picked up on, such as his refusal to have a baby, and the difficulty I had contacting him when he was away on work in Crete, which was all week, every week. But I was immersed in my art and until lately it had been so good to see Panos when he came home that it was almost worth him being away! Having said that he was becoming more distant from me, furthermore I realized that sex had, for him, become an irksome duty not a pleasure.

Then it all came crashing down, Panos was killed in a car accident. I had to go to Thessaloniki to identify his body. That in itself was awful, but much worse was to come. I was told – and this is the really shocking bit – that he had never been working in Crete, but had a woman and two small children in Thessaloniki. I was utterly shocked. This man that I loved and respected had been deceiving me, not just with a wayward fling - that might have been acceptable-- but by living a totally separate life. My whole emotional structure clattered down around me like a house of cards. How could I trust anyone? How could I trust myself? How could I have indulged myself in my art whilst I was being duped by this man.

My dear Nigel, to tell you of all this, to write it on my computer keyboard, is almost more than the courage that I possess. You will realise what a failure I am, what a fool I have been, and how I am so embarrassed by my own gullibility that I have had to retreat from my known world, from Athens and all but one of my friends. Ellie and my brother Lukas are the only people that know of this horrible situation, I have not the courage to tell even my parents. And now I am telling you, but in the full realization that you will think so little of me that you will, politely of course, step back from the brink and withdraw from this budding relationship of ours.

And now my dear Nigel, I will leave my fate, our fate, in your hands.

I am very fond of you, please take care

Anna xx

(Lake District, UK)

It was so good to see Caroline. She had arrived only a little bit later than she expected. Nigel had suggested to Charles that he might like to come and have supper with them, he would love to see Caroline, she was almost an older sister to him. All three of them had rushed out into the drive to greet her. They had settled into the sitting room for a drink with both Caroline and Judith opting for a dry white wine from Alsace, whilst Nigel poured himself a rather over-generous gin, to which he added a somewhat under-generous amount of tonic. Charles sat on the sofa next to Caroline and had a small white wine with a liberal amount of water added to it,

They chatted together catching up on news of themselves and friends. The subject of Caroline's wedding came up briefly. She deftly slipped into the conversation that she and Peter did not want a huge ceremony at home, rather they would prefer a quiet wedding in London with just a few friends. Much to Nigel's relief, Judith did not say a word against the idea indeed at least by omission she seemed to almost welcome it. Mind you he was far from certain that his wife had fully understood what was being said; she seemed to be off again in a dream world of her own.

Nigel had, with a little help from Zenca, done most of the cooking. He had opted for fresh salmon, lightly poached and served with a basil sauce. He was pleased when it was well received by both women. Whilst it was a very newly acquired skill, his cooking was improving all the time.

Caroline confirmed this "Glad to see your cooking's getting better, Nige."

"Not up to your standard yet," he said. Caroline was a first-rate cook. "But better than your mother's ever was!"

"Hey," said Judith, "that was a bit below the belt." She had another glass of wine, probably her sixth or seventh. Not wishing to confront her and start a scene Nigel quietly removed the half empty bottle.

They moved on to sticky toffee pudding with Crème Fraiche. Nigel knew that this was a favourite of his both his wife and Charles. He said as much as he handed Judith her plate.

Judith got to her feet clutching her plate. Her eyes were curiously blank. "God, I hate this stuff," she said. And with that she flung both plate and pudding fiercely onto the carpeted floor. The plate broke into pieces and the pudding scattered itself in blobs over the plain rust-coloured carpet. Judith just stood there, her hands on her hips looking as if nothing had happened. She looked from one to the other of them with an expression of total innocence. "What's the problem?"

"Leave it, Caro," said Nigel as his daughter fell to her knees and started to clear up the mess. He turned to Judith "What the hell did you do that for?"

Judith looked at him with an expression of hurt in her eyes "Do what?"

Caroline looked up at Nigel. "Don't blame her, Nige, she doesn't know that she did it."

"Did what, what did I do. Caroline what are you doing down there. Ugh, what a mess. Charles, did you drop your plate? I hope it won't stain the carpet, you careless boy."

Charles opened his mouth to say something, but Caroline quickly squeezed his hand and he thought better of it.

Zenca had heard the commotion, and rushed in. She quickly realized what had happened and with great efficiency cleared up that which was left of the mess after Caroline's efforts. A large damp patch remained on the carpet, but it looked as if there would be no permanent damage to it.

They all sat down again to finish their meal. Whilst the others were eating their pudding Judith helped herself to a slice of very ripe Brie. Clearly she had seen that Nigel had put the wine bottle in the sideboard cupboard. She retrieved the bottle and washed down with a couple of glasses. "Well then, that's all over. It was a bit of a mess, but I think we have managed to cope pretty well under the circumstances. There really is no need to apologize, Charles these things just happen, it was just unfortunate."

Nigel could take this unfairness no more. "How dare you accuse Charles. You must know that you did this, quite deliberately, not as an accident. The apology due is from you to Charles."

"Don't be ridiculous, Nige, you are just covering up for the boy". And with that she swept from the room.

Caroline gave Charles a big hug. "She's not well, is she?" he asked.

Caroline shook her head "No. and I'm so sorry that you were in the firing line this time."

"No worries," said the lad. "Thanks for supper, the pudding was just great." Nigel and Caroline watched as he hopped on his bike, gave them a cheery wave, and peddled off home.

"No vote of confidence in my salmon then?" His daughter hugged him.

They took their coffee through to the sitting room.

"She's getting worse isn't she Nige?"

"I'm afraid so. It's the combination of her heavy drinking with this bi-polar thing. But it is the drinking that is the real problem. Her social drinking is just the tip of the iceberg. I keep removing bottles of Vodka from the places she hides them, but I'm not winning, and she is getting more cunning all the time."

"What can be done, Nige?"

"Lynn says absolutely nothing until she admits that she has a problem. Only then is it possible to work with her to and to sort her out.

"How long can you cope?"

"Zenca does all the hard graft, and she is very good at coming in and 'baby-sitting' her when I have to go out. But as you have just seen it really is quite a worry to leave her on her own anymore."

"Obviously I'm concerned about Mum, but Nige you really have to look after yourself. It's one hell of an emotional and physical strain on you, and I'm worried about you."

Nigel thought how much more his daughter would be worried if she knew about the relationship – and oh yes it was indeed that – that he was indulging himself in with Anna. Would Caro understand? Perhaps she would realize that this was how he was getting some emotional support? He knew his daughter to be very broad-minded. But then again, she might feel differently about her father getting involved with another woman. She could be okay about it, but he did not want to chance it.

"Where are you, Nige? You've gone off somewhere!"

"Ooops, sorry, just thinking about different times."

"She will have to go into a home, won't she?"

"Not if I can help it, at least not permanently. They're awful places, Caro, loads of old folks sitting around in chairs and waiting for the grim reaper to tell them that they are next in line. Also, I am not sure what home would have her. Quite honestly she is a liability."

Caroline left after a fairly early breakfast. She kissed her mother goodbye and Nigel saw a tear making its way down his daughter's left cheek. He walked with her to her car.

"I'll look after her don't worry."

"Oh, Nige, poor you. This really isn't your thing, is it?"

Nigel shook his head miserably and looked so woebegone that his normally undemonstrative daughter gave him the second big hug of her visit.

"I'll come and see you whenever I can, and I'll tell Jimmy that he should do the same."

As her car swooshed off down the drive, scattering loose pebbles Nigel found that his eyes were watering. He blinked several times and walked slowly back to the house. He was in need of comfort, no not comfort he thought, but comforting – and he knew just where he should turn, where there was a kind and compassionate woman that would provide him with all that he needed.

He read Anna's e-mail with the greatest attention. As he came towards the last part of what she said he was brought up short. Never mind his own problems, Anna had experienced, and was having to face, far worse. There came upon him a sudden and almost unbearable compulsion to fold his arms around this stranger and weep with her. He pulled the keyboard towards him.

My Dearest Anna,
Yes, the waters are indeed getting deeper, for as we tell
each other about our lives, our thoughts and our feelings so

a bond grows between us that I know we can both recognize, no perhaps more than recognize – feel is perhaps the right word for this kind of empathy.

You have told me things that you would only tell, have only told, to someone you care for deeply, and this I find incredibly moving. You have entrusted me with a broken part of your psyche. I am not offering sympathy, although I feel sad for you. I am not offering pity for that is such a negative response.

No, I am simply going to say that you have been through what must be the biggest psychological trauma of your life and you have emerged, as is evident from your e-mails to me, as a strong, empathetic and sensitive person. You have my admiration and, of course, my wholehearted support.

You say that you think of yourself now as a failure and a fool. Nonsense. Just look what you have done. You have started a new life and a new job. Not only do you have absolutely nothing to be ashamed of or embarrassed about but rather you have a lot to congratulate yourself for. And to suggest that I might want to walk away from this deep friendship of ours is so wrong that I almost feel insulted that you could think this of me.

I would love to have seen some of your paintings. You have read my poetry and that is a gateway to my inner thoughts – surely painting was a similar gateway for you? Did you keep any paintings, or better still do you have any photos of them that you could send me?

Being an artist or a poet is a way of venting our over-charged emotional selves, but they are both things that you do in the privacy of your own room, they are lonely occupations and as such it is hardly surprising that we both feel the need for human emotional contact. And now I think that with you I have found just that.

You know my situation regarding Judith and I have told you, perhaps more than I should, about my inability to make serious emotional contact at a personal level. I wonder if that is something that troubles you – it may be an issue of trust

I find much solace in one of my few real passions – that of the English countryside. I feel it is part of my soul. I have only rarely – and for very short periods – lived in a town, and hated it! There is a sort of soul-music in land-scape – not just the aesthetic beauty of it and certainly not the scientific study of it, but rather the layers of history, of social struggle and of individual care that it has and has endured, it is an essential part of my being.

Anna, I have written at some length and find that I keep shying away from the real issue, and I must face up to it or, as you so rightly tell me, I will regret it for the rest of my life. I find myself, totally inexplicably, with a sudden and very strong emotional attachment to you. Does this frighten you? It certainly frightens the hell out of me! We are different people, from different countries and cultures, but there is a force that is pulling us together and I am not sure if I could, or if I want, to resist it.

I fully realize that I may be doing the same as you fear for yourself – that is churning up great clouds of fantasy and enveloping the real you in them so that what I am feeling about you is just a figment of my own creativity. I do however have the greatest of needs for you. I crave your emotional support and so I am driven, despite the reserva-tions of my logical self, to join hands and leap into this relationship with you – I really have no other option– and I do so with a light heart and a happy smile.

Yours very affectionately,
Nigel xxx

11

<u>**(Attika, Greece)**</u>

Anna had thought that the 'day off' for the education strike would be ideal for visiting her parents. She had phoned her mother the previous evening and arranged to be in their village before midday. So here she was, sipping a Greek coffee on the balcony and catching up with all the family news.

"But what about you, dear?" Her mother said. "You cannot possibly manage all by yourself in that remote little cottage of yours."

Anna explained that she was just fine. She told her parents all about the job, and how awful her start had been, but how she would persevere with it. She said that Ellie had been to see her several times, the last with a male friend of hers.

Of course her mother pricked up her ears at the words 'male friend'. "Tell me about him, dear. He isn't Ellie's boyfriend is he?"

"Oh no, just a work colleague. His name is Stergios, he is in his late forties and is a solicitor with the local municipality"

"Is he married?" The inevitable maternal question.

"No, mum, but please don't go getting any ideas."

"Hmmm, a solicitor you tell us," said Anna's father, "A good professional job, and the Municipality means job security, and that means a lot these days."

Anna was concerned about her father. His condition was a good deal worse than it had been only a couple of months ago. He now found it difficult to walk without wheezing, and stairs had become impossible.

"Well," said her mother, "We are so pleased that you have found a nice, respectable, Greek man. It is exactly what you need. No doubt you will be living in Athens?"

Anna looked at her parents. She loved them dearly, but this sort of inquisition and presumption was too much. "No, no, no." she said, "You have got it all wrong."

"Nonsense, baby," said her mother, "Ellie has done very well in introducing you to this nice Greek man, and I am sure you will be very happy with him."

Anna could stand it no longer. "But I have someone else," she blurted out. As soon as the words left her lips she regretted it, why couldn't she just keep quiet.

"Aha!" said her mother. "Do tell us my dear. Where does he live? what does he do? How much does he earn? Who are his parents? How old is he? Has he been married? Does he have any children Is he a widower?"

"Really mother, you are impossible. Do you expect me to tell you everything about every man I meet?"

"Now Anna," said her father. "Your mother is just asking for your own good, so don't answer her back like that."

"Okay," said Anna. "You really want to know about Nigel?" She took a deep breath, "then I will tell you. He is English. He is rather more than ten years older than I am. He is married with two grown up children. I have never met him face to face, but met him on the internet. I am very fond of him, and he of me."

"Anna! How Could you." Shrieked her mother. "What are you thinking of."

Anna's father had turned a deathly white and the sweat was standing out on his face. "My pills," he croaked.

Her mother grabbed a bottle off the buffet whilst Anna rushed into the kitchen for a glass of water. When she returned her father had lost consciousness and slumped towards the floor. Her mother phoned for an ambulance whilst Anna lay him flat and put a cushion under his legs. His eyes fluttered and Anna told him not to try to talk.

Less than an hour later Anna and her mother were sitting in a green-walled waiting area in the Chalkis General Hospital. A young doctor walked briskly into the room, a stethoscope around her neck. "Your husband has had an episode brought on by a sudden reduction in blood pressure. This is usually due to a fall, or possibly a severe shock. He will be fit enough to go home in an hour or so, but I must insist that he is kept calm and is not subjected to anything that might agitate him."

As the doctor left Anna's mother turned on her. "You stupid, stupid girl. You very nearly killed him. You and your smart ways, you think you know everything and are so much better than the rest of us. No wonder Panos left you for another woman."

It was Anna's turn to be shocked. "How did you know that? I never told you anything."

"You didn't have to, everyone knows, it is the talk of the village. Have you not brought enough shame on our family by being incapable of keeping a good man as your husband? So now you are in some crazy adventure with a foreigner who has a wife."

"I haven't met him. It is just conversation on the internet."

"Don't you see? That makes it even worse. You have no idea who this man is, who his parents are, and if he is genuine. Anna, this is too bad. Why can't you find some nice, respectable Greek man and settle down with him."

"Mum, I love you both dearly, and I don't want to cause you worry. I know you only have my best interests at heart and I am desperately sorry about what just happened with Dad. But Mum, I am a grown woman and I have to find the way that is right for me. I know that with Nigel I am following my heart and not my head, but that is how it is. I would prefer to make a genuine mistake rather than fall again into the sort of situation I had with Panos."

Anna ensured that her father was brought back home and comfortably put into his bed. She kissed both her parents, and with a great lump in her throat wished them all her love before leaving.

As she drove home, she cried. Was she really so bad a person as her mother made out? Had she really nearly killed her father? And what for? A bit of self-indulgence over the ether. She was indeed a despicable person.

(Evia, Greece)

-

> *Dear Nigel,*
>
> *I am so ashamed of myself. It has been wrong of me to indulge myself in your kindness and warmth and to lead you on by telling you that I have become deeply attached to you.*
>
> *There are situations in life, external pressures that are beyond our control, and expectations of others that militate against relationships that are out of the ordinary.*
>
> *Yesterday I was goaded into revealing something of our relationship to my parents. My mother, bless her, was oh so upset. But worse my father, who as I think I have told you, suffers from ill health, had a nasty turn and we had to get him to hospital.*

*I know that I am a bad person, selfish and hot-headed.
I can only say how sorry I am, and how much, my dear
Nigel, I will miss our intimate correspondence.
With heartfelt sorrow
Anna*

(Lake District, UK)

Nigel had been out the whole day. He had, perhaps rather misguidedly, started a business selling electric motor conversions for diesel-powered craft. He had recently sold such a conversion to a firm who operated on the Norfolk Broads and his presence was needed for final trials of the system. A very early start had ensured arrival at Wroxham by 10.30 in the morning. Things had gone well, and after a late lunch at a pub in Horning Nigel was able to get back to the Lake District by 7 o'clock in the evening.

He was exhausted but he checked on Judith to find that she was reclining in the conservatory, fast asleep. Zenca told him that she had been pretty quiet most of the day, except when Lakeland Landscapes asked her for instructions about her water feature. She had told them to go and jump in it!

Tired as he was, he sat down by his computer in the hope that Anna had written to him. Good, she had. He opened her e-mail and read it.

For a long time he sat and did nothing, his mind a blank, his chest a great hollow of misery.

She was right of course. Her parents were right. No doubt her friend Ellie was right. He was an old, married, foreigner whom she had never met and to whom she was pouring out her most intimate thoughts. Furthermore he in his turn was burdening her with his hang-ups and his marital problems. The situation was intolerable.

With the greatest reluctance he pulled the keyboard towards him.

> *Dear Anna,*
>
> *I do of course blame myself. It is I who have led us into this unhappy situation and I must take responsibility for it. We should never have come this far. It is unforgivable of me.*
>
> *Please do not think for one more minute that you are a 'bad person'. You are the most courageous, uplifting, honest and loving person that I have been privileged to know. You are also so sensitive to the mores of others that you are willing to abandon your own feelings. Whilst from my personal perspective that is utterly disappointing, it is also a measure of your strength.*
>
> *Had our circumstances been different then all might have been well. We would have met each other and, in the conventional way, would have had a chance to get to know each other properly.*
>
> *I suppose it might be possible to keep in touch on a friendly basis? But no, I am not sure that I could manage that. There is only so much emotional repression that even an Englishman can take.*
>
> *So, kisses, my Anna, and every kind wish to you for the future.*
> *Nigel*

He read his short e-mail several times. Whilst his whole instinct was to delete it and send a loving note to Anna, his conscience and his duty towards her dictated otherwise. He had, in pursuing her this far, expected her to reject much of her culture. It was considered immoral in her country to have a relationship with a married man, even if for a widow. It was also 'unseemly' for even a mature woman to behave against the wishes of her parents. He could not be responsible for her flouting convention.

After much hesitation and the most severe misgivings he clicked 'Send'.

He felt awful. A gigantic hole had opened up in his life and swallowed all that was good. He wandered rather aimlessly out of the study. He could not face his wife. Pulling on an old Barbour jacket against the rapidly deteriorating weather he headed out of the house.

(Evia, Greece)

-

Had Nigel written in any other way Anna would have accepted the situation for what it was. However, he took the full responsibility upon himself. He did not blame her, indeed on the contrary he was kind and understanding of her situation. What is more he made no attempt to get her to change her mind. This was the very antithesis of male dominance, of arrogant selfishness.

She thought of how Panos might have treated her in similar circumstances. It would have amounted to verbal bullying. Whatever he would have wanted he would have been determined to have his own way and she would have been expected to comply.

Here, with Nigel, was partnership, equality, personal responsibility. She knew that this is what she had missed so much in her marriage. Here it was in the form of a disembodied foreigner. What should she do? Was she really prepared to give up this man because of the petty conventions of village life? Yet she cared so deeply for her parents that she felt unable to go against their express wishes.

She phoned Ellie.

"You behaved decently towards your parents," said Ellie, "but in doing so you have screwed up this relationship that I really think might have been going somewhere."

"But I cannot get away from the fact that Nigel is married. Not happily married, but nevertheless he has an alcoholic wife that he feels he has a duty to care for."

"That is a problem. But as you have not met him, and are unlikely to do so, I hardly think that you can be accused of having an 'affair' with a married man."

"Perhaps not physically, although I might like that very much, but certainly emotionally."

"That does not count in the eyes of the world – thank goodness!"

"And the other thing is that he is English. My parents are upset about that. They cannot see why I need to take up with a foreigner."

"Frankly, Anna, nor do I. But you have, and there is no undoing what is in your heart."

"I really don't know what to do."

Ellie replied that only she, Anna, could make that decision. Nigel would not make contact again and if she did not make contact with him then her friendship with him was at an end.

"Anyway," said Ellie, 'We will meet again soon and you can tell me what you decided.

Anna lit one cigarette after another. She had to resolve matters and whilst Ellie had tried to be helpful she could hardly have expected Ellie to make her decisions for her. She sat at her table and tentatively opened up her laptop.

Dearest Nigel,

This is so difficult for me to write, for I feel that I am such a fool.

Your last e-mail was all that I could have expected of you. You took the blame for everything and you said that I was courageous, honest and loving. I don't feel anything like that just at present. I feel depressed, guilty and stupid. I keep changing my mind every two minutes and I don't know what I can possibly say to you.

What I do know is that I cannot bear to lose your intimate friendship. However here in Greece the biggest problem are parents! They are so intrusive, and they ask questions that you dare not even ask of yourself. In my case I only had to mention your name and they wanted to find out if you were suitable marriageable material! In a way this must seem amusing to you, but believe me it is not so funny when you have to live with it.

So, my parents consider you to be 'the man in my life' whether or not I consider you to be such, and certainly without considering you in the matter. This means that according to the cultural rule book of rural Greece you must conform to certain standards. You should 'tick a number of boxes'. In particular you should be Greek, of good professional standing, have socially acceptable family connections and, of course, be unmarried.

Most of those boxes you do not tick, and as a result my family are desperately upset about what I, what we, are doing. I have to face these obstacles, well we both do. You cannot help being English, any more than you can change your age. Furthermore you are likely to remain married for a good long time. You are therefore regarded almost as an outcast, and certainly not suitable material for me!

Having said all that can't help but tell you how pleased, indeed happy I am every time I receive your messages. And running the risk of your thinking that I might be mentally damaged, ""``Also, I sort of "know" when an e-mail from you reaches my Inbox.

Nigel, my feeling towards this strange relationship of ours is of essential importance to me, although I don't know why. And I don't want to lose it. Your voice that reaches through the screen of my computer speaks as if it were a voice that I've known for a long time. It is like a scent that subtly accompanies a precious moment or a happy part of life that has been registered and kept in the subconscious for a long, long time, so that once you happen to come across it again, perhaps many years later, it reminds you of something that is so hard to define. It fills you with an emotion that you cannot recognize for you can't remember where it originates.

She would have liked have added "are you so blind not to see that I'm flying high at every single word you write to me?" but of course to write this would be going well beyond their current state of intimacy .

One more glass of wine was consumed, and another cigarette was lit. "Very well then, what exactly is your interest in me then, my dear?" Nigel could ask in his upper middle-class British way. But there was no answer to that. No answer that came to mind.

Well by now you will have had enough of me. Just a few hours ago we had almost 'signed off' with each other, and here

am I holding out my heart to you on a plate. If you want my intimate friendship then it is all yours.
Please reply soon, even if it is to reject this plea.
With fondest wishes
Anna xx

(Lake District, UK)

My very Dearest Anna,

I had just reconciled myself to never hearing from you again and have spent the last hour and a half in the local pub bemoaning the fate of the male of the species, without unduly praising the distaff side – and here you are!

I find it hard to know what to say. I do of course welcome you, heart and all, into my life. I would find it a colourless and dull existence without your e-mails bounding across the continent to land in my computer. However I can understand your parents' concerns, and that of the society that they are part of. The thing is that in so many ways they are right, and the sad position I find myself in is that there is so little that I can do to change things.

As you so rightly point out I cannot alter the fact that I am and Englishman. I suppose I could dye the grey bits in my hair, forge my birth certificate and lose ten years. But that seems rather pathetic. But most of all I am married to Judith. This is pretty well non-negotiable, on the other hand it is hardly an impediment to our exchanging thoughts and feelings with each other by e-mail. I do not feel that I am letting her down in seeking solace elsewhere, however although Judith and I have not had sex for nearly two years now I do think it would be wrong of me to deceive her physically. Don't get me wrong my dear, I am speaking hypothetically, I am not suggesting that we are missing out on an illicit sexual liaison, just clarifying my own thoughts on infidelity.

I am far from clear as to where this leaves us. But I would suggest that we neither kill this relationship stone dead, nor rush into each other's arms. Let us take things slowly and enjoy each other's company as best we can
Yours very affectionately
Nigel

(Evia, Greece)

-

Anna was initially disappointed in Nigel's response. Whilst in places it showed that he had deep feelings for her there was a coldness about the style of writing, as if he had withdrawn, at least in part, from their relationship.

Her belief was that everyone has their share in life of the things that they truly wish for. She and Nigel were very much alike in terms of creativity and emotional needs, but had lived their creative lives as a mirror image of each other.

For a very large part of her life she had been able to express herself creatively though her art, but she no longer felt able to do that. Conversely Nigel not been able to allow his creativity to flourish for a substantial part of his life but now felt free to do so.

She felt that both of them now had a far greater knowledge and understanding of the traumas that the other had been through. Indeed Nigel had given her such confidence in all that he had said about her reaction to the crisis that had enveloped her life. She had been so relieved by his attitude. Fearing that he would see it quite differently.

Now, however things had changed, and it needed time and a lot of work before some sort of resolution could be achieved,

The clock on the computer showed that it was getting very late but it was not beyond normal bedtime yet. She had to wake up first thing in the morning to face yet another challenging day of confrontation at work, but this was the most important part of her day and it deserved some celebration; a glass of local red Chardonnay and a cigarette. It was, for early March, a comparatively mild night, but not as yet warm enough to be able to take the laptop outside into the yard. She could do with opening a window. It was a wonderfully clear night with the stars shining brightly above her. She was so lucky that the lights of the village were far enough away not to spoil her enjoyment of the night sky. The moon was emerging from behind the mountains and in a while a whole section of the stars would not be visible anymore, overshadowed by the queen of the sky, the brightest Pale of all. She smiled as she remembered Nigel's poem. If nothing else they seemed to be equals in their love of the Moon.

She wrote:

> *Dearest Nigel,*
>
> *I cannot answer your welcome e-mail directly, it is not that sort of evening, all I can do is to try to put into words a few of my inner feelings.*
>
> *When I read your e-mails I find a man who is oozing with understanding and kindness.*
>
> *You are good with words. You conjure with them, cajoling them to emerge as beautiful, sweet-sounding, music arranged effectively into verses and sentences that gave a deep, compact meaning to such a small handful of typewritten letters. But it is*

not this ability with form that appeals to my soul, perhaps it is not even the meaning of the words. It is the sense of them, a feeling of such proximity that is in striking contrast to the distance and the differences between you and me.

Perhaps I am taking the easy-way out. It is unlikely that I will ever know you in person, and most probably will never see what you look you like, or how you speak, or what expression your face would take when saying certain things. I will most probably never know if the kind persona of your emails is just as kind in reality. Perhaps this 2,500km barrier between us is what attracts us to each other? Relating to each other from the safety of our own homes without running the risk of getting to know each other in the flesh, thereby failing and hurting each other?

Words... They could most certainly be beautiful, but then that could be all that they are - just Words.

Very fondly yours,

Anna

She knew in her heart that she was falling for Nigel. He had a wife he seemed to genuinely care for, although hardly out of romantic love. In real life, this would automatically forbid her from moving into any serious involvement with him. But now, what was this wife? She was just words on the virtual page of a computer screen; such an image of a woman, of a wife, could never be real. He had said that Judith was suffering from alcoholism and some side effects, but then how could she, Anna, be sure of that?

There were plenty of husbands who had sustained affairs for years on end and had come up with all sorts of lies about their wives. It was ironic that she had quite obviously married one of exactly that type. But then, was Nigel any more real than his wife? Perhaps it just suited her and perhaps she was swimming in self-delusion, but in her heart she knew that he was real. Perhaps more real than many other things she had thought of as being so. But then, how could she ever be sure?

She could have gone on writing to him for the rest of the night, but this had already become a much longer message than intended. Would he read it tonight? Was he expecting it?

Anna did not switch off the computer. It was getting quite late now and though by this the time that she would normally be going to sleep, yet she was not the least bit sleepy. She was disturbed and felt vulnerable because of what she had just written. She put on a cardigan and went outside. The quiet night enveloped her, the smells from the garden, and the darkness, the towering outline of the mountains illuminated by the moon. They were all so reassuring, confirming that she was consciously and sanely still of this world. But they answered no questions as she stood there, staring into the night, for some considerable time.

(Lake District, UK)

-

Dearest Anna,

A moment ago I was sitting here at my desk in a somewhat melancholy mood, wondering what to do about Judith and whether I should continue with this poetry thing which seemed to be causing me more emotional turmoil rather than relieving me of such. And then suddenly my whole evening was brightened by your e-mail arriving, newborn as it were, straight from its conception in your mind.

I am becoming even more worried about Judith. She had another bad do yesterday evening when my daughter Caroline was with us. It was nothing too awful, just a broken

> *plate, but she is suffering these moments of temporary black-out quite frequently. I struggle to do this caring thing. It is not a skill that comes easily to me. I may have to get some live-in help, our Polish girl, Zenca, is very good with Judith and is so helpful at coming in and looking after her when I am out, but she has her own young family to look after – and I think Judith is going to need more time than Zenca can offer.*

Nigel read Anna's e-mail again, twice. It was almost a love-letter. She talked obliquely about her feelings for him. He was certain that she held true deep feelings towards him.

OK, so he was the great rationalist. It was fine analyzing her feelings for him, how about being a bit more honest about himself? He shut his eyes and let his mind delve deep into his inner being. In his imagination he found a small thing curled up under a great mountain. He prodded it gently with a finger. The thing slowly uncurled, and like a butterfly emerging from a chrysalis a beautiful golden, shimmering being appeared. There was no doubt in his mind that it was a woman, but it was so bright that he could make out no clear form, and certainly no distinguishable facial features. It seemed to hover just clear of the indistinct surface, glowing softly, sometimes brightly, sometimes quite dimly, its intensity changing as if it were the beating of a heart. And Nigel could feel within him, from where this vision emanated, a wonderful warm glow, a deep passionate longing, an understanding of an absolute harmony.

He reached out to try to touch this thing of beauty, but without seeming to move it withdrew from his outstretched arm. He knew that it was not yet his to touch. His head was filled with the most glorious music, not loud, just all embracing. It was a kind of Gregorian chant, but exuding a sense of playfulness and laughter as well as a feeling of spirituality and devotion. And as he bathed in the wonder of this thing it slowly faded from his eyes, seeming to just evaporate, but as it did so it reached out an arm that he could see with clarity, and its hand was beckoning him to follow.

Nigel opened his eyes. He was trembling slightly. 'Bloody hell, what the devil was that.' But in his heart he knew what it was, even though it was an emotion that he had never felt before. He turned back to his keyboard.

I really want to talk about my own personal feelings. The very strong, very deep feelings that I have for you. I think I am just ducking the issue by chattering on about anything else, and that is because I am embarrassed and uneasy about my own emotions. You really only have yourself to blame in that you set me upon this track of 'carpe diem'. That is to say that if I do not roll with whatever life offers me then I will miss out on it forever.

I am talking, my dear Anna, about our relationship. I have been trying not to name my strong emotional attachment to you because I am so worried about it, and I am even more worried about 'coming clean' to you that I have these feelings. I have a wife for whom I have an ongoing responsibility and our circumstances of age and distance are such as to totally rule out anything other than a 'virtual relationship – and I have very little clear idea of what that might mean.

He had gone too far. Surely Anna would read what he had just written and bolt like a startled rabbit. What right had he to force his imagining upon a vulnerable woman? Well either he did, and suffer the consequences, or he did not and would be forever unsure about what that daydream of his was really about. He had no option; he had to go on

> *Now that I have, as it were, opened up my feelings to you I feel very vulnerable, also very fearful in that over the past week I have enjoyed and treasured this friendship that has grown up between us and the very last thing that I want to do is for you to take fright and disappear back into the ether from whence you have come. I feel that you are a strong person, but with vulnerabilities. I am a man with all sorts of emotional baggage that you could not possibly want to carry, and yet I do not deny that I am asking you to (virtually!) hold my hand and walk with me into the unknown. That is neither decent nor fair.*

How he should go on from here? It was as if he was a schoolboy penning a note to his first love. He needed to steady his nerves. The whisky bottle rattled against the cut glass as he poured himself a generous tot. Here he was again, drinking alone, but perhaps he was no longer alone. There on the screen Anna had been communicating with him, true she was not flesh and blood, but she was openness and emotion and that was, at the very least companionable. It was getting quite late. He clicked open the 'dashboard' on his iMac and the clock app. He entered 'Europe' and the 'Athens', the clock swivelled. Hmmmmm, it would be two hours later there – the small hours of the night. Surely she would have gone to bed? He took another slug at the whisky, almost draining the glass. He would finish at that.

> *Your very affectionate and loving,*
> *Nigel*

This was not an e-mail to ponder upon, to spell-check, to re-read, to amend, to curtail. This was something raw and untried, a breasting of an emotion that had carried him through the writing of it since he had experienced that day-dream. He drained the last few dregs of whisky out of his glass whilst at the same time he hit Send.

12

Anna was calmer when she returned in the house but as she approached her laptop with the intention of switching off, she automatically hit the connection button. She was surprised to see Nigel's name in the new messages. She looked at the time he had sent it. It read 'Now'.

It was getting really late now, far beyond her usual bed time, and she was only too aware that she had to go to school the next day, although fortunately her the timetable scheduled her for only a couple of hours teaching fairly late on. She was astonished at how fast this new job, which she had looked forward to with such pleasurable anticipation and that she had started with such enthusiasm, was turning out to be just a cruel disillusionment, turning so quickly into nothing more than an unbearable exercise in drudgery. But there were only a couple of months left until the end of the school-year and if she took into account all the teachers' meetings and seminars and elections and excursions and strikes, she doubted there was more than a month of actual teaching. She found these thoughts distasteful but she could not be sure whether she was disgusted at the situation or at herself for thinking like this. She pushed these annoying thoughts out of her mind. She looked at her screen. There was Nigel's new message, and it opened up a whole new perspective, taking her to unvisited territory, revealing a totally unprecedented Nigel. This was another world.

She indulged herself in every single word of his message. Trembling slightly she let it spread and melt within her; she slowly sipped his words in the same manner that she would have sipped her favourite very expensive, silk-textured, fruit and flower-scented red wine. And when she finished reading, she went through it again, and then again. Until she could almost recite every word he had written, until she had captured and considered every meaning he that had put across, every implication.

She impulsively hit on the reply button.

She should have waited until the next morning. She was over-emotional now and what would he think of her responding to him so late in the night? He would, quite rightly, imagine that she was hanging around just staring at her computer screen awaiting his reply. She looked at the blank space her message would occupy. Her mind told her that it was not wise to write something at this time of night and whilst she felt so emotional. But she seldom listened to her mind. How could she just go and sleep after receiving such a communication? She was made of different stuff.

> *My dearest Nigel,*
>
> *I have just read your beautiful message and I can't possibly tell you how my heart leaps within my breast, how it is overflowing with a feeling of togetherness, of one-ness with you, my Nigel. I know how deeply I feel for you. I have been wrestling with this feeling for some time, although not for the most part consciously. I have too been trying to deny it, both because my mind has been telling me that it is irrational but also, because I could feel you shying away from it. I understand your concerns, your fears, your*

reservation, because I have little doubt that they are very similar to mine.

I also have a whole pantheon of fears that I struggle to deal with every single day in an attempt to ensure that I rule my own life, not be ruled by these untoward emotions.

Nigel, I am aware that I'm rather surprising you right now, for you were afraid that I would be scared by learning of your own feelings and that I would turn my back on you However instead of that just look what I'm coming up with! But I would be such a terrible liar, such a pathetic coward if I did not share with you what seems to overwhelm me, becoming more and more intense each passing day, more urgent and undeniable with each of your incoming messages.

I don't really have any answers to give you. I am at a loss. What this sense of familiarity is or where it comes from, and whether it's real or a dream we see together – I don't know. But I know how I feel. I know you have become very important to me., my darling.

Anna stopped to take a breath. She had written these words as if she was in a trance, and at such speed that her mail application might almost be sweating to keep up with her. It was as if her hands had acquired a life of their own and did not need her rational thought, nor her control anymore. She wrote as if she was totally disengaged from any form of defensive logic. She looked at the "my darling" with which she had finished her sentence. It appeared as if it was a beacon, calling for her attention. Too late now, she had opened this Pandora's Box and she could not go back, nor did she wish to. If there was a speck of truth in what she or Nigel felt for each other then it was best that they should bring it right out into the open.

So, what's going to happen now? You offer me your virtual hand to take and I follow you to the unknown? I think I have just taken it in mine, although I am now quite certain that I don't like virtual relationships. It's not the unknown that scares me; it's the impersonal, even when it becomes as personal as it has just got. Besides, I genuinely wonder, what do people do in virtual relationships? I have no idea, but perhaps you do? Do they exchange the day's news, do they tell each other loving things, do they have sex in words? These are just the few possibilities that my imagination can come up with. Perhaps you will say to me that it is nothing more than that which we have already been doing. But that just wouldn't be good enough, would it? Sure, our e-mail exchanges have been great in establishing a friendship between us but although I do indeed have friendly feelings for you, these are not the ones that really matter to me anymore.

She paused again. Her writing had continued to precede her thinking. But now, it was as if an alarm bell had sounded in her mind. Nigel had admitted that she was not indifferent to him, and had acknowledged that she was not a selfish person; he had realised that she cared about him far beyond a pen-pal friendship level, but he had at the same time expressed serious doubt, if not negative certainty, as to whether she would be willing to have anything to do with his "emotional baggage". That seemed so contradictory. Of course he might have said so whilst in reality just looking for reassurance, just angling for her to come back and tell him how much she cared about him. Yes, this could be his way of prying for her true feelings. But she was not utterly convinced by that, for if she combined it with his apparent certainty that theirs could not be anything other than a virtual relationship - oh how she had come to despise that phrase - then where did that leave them? Might this be all that it could be to Nigel? Was there a possibility that he could not go beyond straightforward verbal communication; that he was incapable of relating to a real person? He had expressed certain concerns about the situation in her country but had then declared that there was really nothing he could do, apart from writing a poem. She squeezed her mind to remember. Had Nigel ever expressed real concern for her? Oh God, it was really late and she was desperately tired and she wondered if she might be becoming seriously paranoid; of course he had. Had he not? Why had she fallen for him for then? Yes, she could remember now, it was his concern and his kind nature that had attracted her in the first place. She relaxed. She breathed with relief. She was so happy to return to her loving thoughts about him. But then again, how much did just a couple of kind words and a little concern cost from such a distance? Oh, she was definitely getting paranoid. If she denied Nigel that, she denied the true nature of what she claimed she felt; and that would negate everything that might resemble love, straight away. Yet she was in love with him, there was no doubt in her mind about that.

> *Unlike you, I need too many words to express my-self - unlucky you! I hope I have not tired you, and I hope that I have not made you feel uncomfortable. Nigel, if you read this carefully, you will get a great deal of information about who I am, what I want and what I hope for. I know you have a sharp mind and you won't miss it. Now, at last, I will send this*

*to you, and to say goodnight I will give you a virtual
stroke of that hand you offered me.*
With my overwhelming affection,
Anna

She hit the sent button, without even checking for spelling mistakes. It was not out of carelessness or negligence. If she were to read again that which she had written she might regret it, back off, erase. But if this relationship, these feelings, were indeed as deep as they seemed to be getting, then she would not hold back from allowing them to go even deeper. She had never liked the surface, anyway. She had a peculiar feeling now. It was not the happiness and the excitement that she had experienced in reading Nigel's message. It was as if there was an insinuation of a tiny hole into her heart, or at least a threat of such a wound. She was really worried about how he would respond to this, but she could not afford to think about it any longer. It was late and her eyes burnt from lack of sleep, the glare from the computer screen, and the intensity of her thoughts and her feelings. She switched off and went to bed. She slept immediately and dreamed an anxiety-ridden dream, of a man that could have been Nigel.

(Lake District, UK)

-

Nigel stifled a yawn. Despite, or perhaps because of, the whisky he found that he just could not relax. Bed was out of the question although it was fast approaching midnight. He thought about Anna in Greece. It woould be the best part of 2 am there, but he was quite certain that she was still awake. He was waiting, waiting for the reply that he knew would come and that would tell him whether he had misjudged the situation utterly, or if Anna felt the same way about him as he did about her. Blast it, he hardly even knew what the woman looked like, and yet he had fallen for her.

He wondered if Internet Relationships were of a purer kind that more conventional ones despite their bad reputation. If he felt this way about someone he had never seen then it almost totally removed the physical, the sexual, element in the relationship. It meant that his feelings for her were mental, emotional, he almost thought 'spiritual'. It was a strange New World that they now inhabited and one that he doubted he was fully equipped to understand. His childhood had been so different from . . .

And then it came. There was a 'ping' from his computer and the Mac Mail icon was registering one incoming message. With a flutter in his heart he opened Anna's message.

He sat quite still reading it, almost consuming it. This was more than he could possibly have expected. This delightful woman was saying quite clearly that she held him very dear. Was it fear, or excitement, or something else? He did not know, but he did realize that he was quite overcome by emotion. He shut his eyes and, perhaps a little too briefly, he thought through the consequences of what he proposed to do. Anna was right. They had to see each other, and not just in photographic images or online communication. They needed to look into each other's eyes, touch each other's flesh, and understand by intonation and inflexion what it was that the other was saying. Certainly it would be possible to continue to exchange e-mails, but where would that get them. She was perspicacious, this Greek woman and despite her rather weird ideas about sensing each other's presence she could see quite clearly what was good and what was not so good about their situation.

He would reply to her straight away. She would have gone to bed by now, for goodness sake she had a job to go to in the morning, but he wanted to say the few words that he had to, and he wanted to send them to her tonight.

My Darling Anna,

I am overwhelmed by a wonderful warm, feeling. It comes from the words that you have written in your e-mail and in particular your saying how much I mean to you.

I am not very good at this sort of thing. All my life I have dealt with tangible things. Things I can see and touch and hear and taste and smell. Your presence on the internet is really none of these – it is just a concept, and however wonderful and inspiring and kind the words are that you write they are just that – like a poem written in a book, open to interpretation by the reader. What I am saying is that we have to meet. I realize that you would find it difficult to come to the UK just now so that means that I must travel to Greece, and if you wish me to do that I will do so.

I think I had better say openly now that I would like to stay with you, and if it seems right after we have met, to sleep with you, by which I mean having sex. I say this so that there is no falseness between us. It is not a 'plan', but if things follow a natural loving course then it is a foregone consequence

If this sounds OK to you just send me the briefest of notes in the morning and I will sort things out. In the meantime I have little doubt that you are soundly asleep – so sleep well, my dear Anna.

With much affection,
Nigel

The following morning dawned bright and clear, a lovely spring day. Nigel eased himself gently out of bed. He pulled on a pair of old trousers, a check shirt and a rather tatty sweater, looked in on his sleeping wife, and. and went in search of coffee.

Mug in hand he walked quickly from the kitchen into the den. The Mac sprang to life at his touch of the space bar and there, sure enough, was an e-mail from Anna:

My dearest Nigel,

This is just a quick note before I leave for work. I will write a full reply soon as I am back.

I was right in thinking that you do indeed have a sharp mind. And I was delighted. Yes, I do want to meet you, to me this would be the proof that this is not a dream that I am seeing whilst awake, but that you really exist and all these wonderful things I have sensed and understood about you, are not just figments of my imagination.

Your wish to stay with me, has taken me aback a little. I don't know why, but I had never thought about our relationship in practical terms. But yes, I would really like that.

Nigel, I am afraid I can't pre-arrange, I can't make a promise as to what will happen when we meet. Yes, if we feel that it is right then we will make love together, but it would be foolish of either of us to make false promises.

This does not, in any way, diminish my desire to see you and to be with you and neither should it make you doubt that. I am just like this. I am looking forward to this moment, and I am open to what it might bring along, but I cannot pre-destine it.

I'll come back with details regarding how we meet when you come. I've got to run now!
I am so excited, and yes, very happy.
Yours with much affection,
Anna

Thinking was best done away from the house and its distractions. He pulled on some boots and set out towards the woodland.

The tree cover was sparse enough to allow almost full sunlight to penetrate the canopy and reach the ground. Nigel had been walking for nearly an hour but for once he hardly took any notice of the landscape through which he was making his way with a firm and determined stride.

For a large part of his walk he had been regretting the impetuosity of his second e-mail to Anna last night. He accepted that his emotional state was such that he was in a vulnerable frame of mind and could be, indeed had been, easily led. He considered his responsibilities, especially to Judith. He was consumed by his own sense of guilt. What the hell did he think he was doing, leaving his wife, even for a few days, to consummate an affair with this lovely Greek woman who was nearly young enough to be his daughter?

Mind you he readily admitted that Anna was pretty good-looking and what was more there was certainly a serious emotional and intellectual bond between them. Even he, Nigel, the doyen of the un-romantics, could feel the spark, the electricity that flowed between him and Anna. She was intelligent, intellectually acute and emotionally aware. 'Bugger it,' he thought hopelessly, 'I am indeed hopelessly fond of her.' But then how stupid was that. For Christ's sake he hadn't even met the woman.

Nigel had turned off the broad forest path and had made his way along a simple trod that meandered its way through oak trees. He followed it, crossing the occasional small beck and noticing the hazel branches left drying, stacked against the trees, by the charcoal burners. In just a month the area would be covered with bluebells, he must remember to come up here again at that time. He came to a step-over stile that led him out of the woodland and into a series of undulating pasture fields surrounded by stone walls.

He felt the duty and responsibility of caring for his wife. What right had he to abandon this woman with whom he had shared so much of his life? He was under no illusion that the outcome of a meeting with Anna might lead to just that. Judith had borne their children, had made their home, had worked with him to establish their business. He had no right whatsoever to go off chasing will-o-the-wisps in some foreign country just because he felt an emotional stirring that he had never encountered before.

Nigel quickened his stride. He would return home and e-mail Anna. He did not want to cause her distress, and he had no intention of ending their relationship, just of slowing things down a little, buying some time. He would be affectionate but he was resolute.

He heard a siren in the distance and wondered idly if it were police, fire or ambulance. There had been a lot of police activity this last month, but the ambulance seemed to have been rather up-staged by the air-ambulance helicopter service. The footpath joined the small country lane that would take him almost to his front door. The hedge was a curious mixture of very old slate slabs and hawthorn bushes. The slabs had been part of the estate boundary of the Furness Abbey lands. They interlocked at the top and at the bottom. Wrostling slates they were called, he supposed it to be a corruption of 'wrestling'. A few years ago a local man had obtained funding to construct some replacements to repair damaged sections and had been moderately successful in getting the local quarry to help him in his venture.

As he turned into his drive Nigel was shocked to see an ambulance at his front door. He ran towards it. It could only be for Judith, and indeed it was. By the time he got there a stretcher bearing his wife had been slipped into the vehicle.

"What's going on? What's happened to her?"

A man with a green and buff uniform bearing the legend 'Paramedic' caught him by the arm. 'Mr. Marston?"

"Yes. But that's my wife. What's happened?"

"Your wife seems to have had a bit of a fall. As far as we can see nothing's broken, but she is bruised and a bit confused. We are taking her to the General, you can ride with her in the ambulance if you want to."

"No, I'll follow you." Nigel did not want to be stuck in town without a car. He saw Zenca standing quietly composed, and a little apart from the action. He went over to her, "Zenca, what happened."

"I found her when I came in. She was in the corridor from the den, I think she had tripped on that step. She was awake but I could not make her understand me, so I called the emergency service and they sent an ambulance. She seems a good deal better already.

"Well done, Zenca, it cannot have been easy for you,"

"No problem."

"That bloody step!"

"I think she had been in the den, it's a bit of a mess in there."

Nigel was torn between following his wife immediately or seeing what she had been up to in his study just before she fell. He opted for the later. "I'll follow you in a moment," he said to the paramedic, and walked into the house.

The den had indeed been left in a chaos, almost as if struck by a whirlwind. Nigel saw that all the things that had been on his desk, pens, filing trays, stapler, calculator and of course his papers had been swept onto the floor. Only his iMac remained. He walked over to it. Scrawled across the screen in a deep red lipstick of Judith's shade was a single word 'BASTARD'. He clicked on the mouse and it was immediately clear to him that Judith had been reading that last, intimate, e-mail exchange between Anna and himself. So, Judith knew. He could imagine her rage as she swept everything to the floor and scrawled upon his computer screen, then, possibly yelling his name, rushed down the corridor to that fateful step.Nigel felt like the creep that he was. Not man enough to keep his emotions in check he had succumbed to a fantasy of his own making about a woman in Greece. He did not blame Anna, indeed he still thought of her with the greatest fondness, but he did blame himself. Shortly he would have to follow Judith to hospital, but first he had another duty to perform, this time to a woman some 1600 miles away. He wiped the lipstick off the screen.

> *My dearest Anna,*
>
> *I have been agonising about your parents' concerns over your relationship with me, a married man. I am quite clear that I have behaved abominably in pursuing you whilst I am still married. I have also not behaved very well to my wife who even now is in hospital. Unfortunately Judith read our last e-mails and must have been in a state of considerable distress which led to a very nasty fall. I am just off to follow her ambulance to hospital.*
>
> *You will appreciate that this rather changes our plans, for whilst I admit I do not love me wife I do feel that I have*

a degree of responsibility towards her, a sentiment that I can only hope you will understand and accept.

I don't know what we should do now, but think we need time to sort things out, and rushing into meeting, and possibly physical love-making would I fear, be premature. Please understand that I still feel the very deepest affection for you. We need to take things slowly, we need more time.

With much affection,

Nigel.

Three hours later Nigel was back home again. Judith had been well sedated and the Hospital wanted to keep her in for twenty-four hours for observation. It appeared that she had suffered nothing more than a fall, leaving her bruised but not harmed in any other way. It was clear that she would be fit enough to return home the next day. Nigel rather shied away from the thought of collecting her. She would have a lot to say to him.

He sat in the empty house and realized just what a mess he had made of his life. His wife was unlikely ever to forgive him for his 'attempted infidelity', and the stress that he had caused her would most likely add to the distress that she was already in because of her condition.

Meanwhile he had at least half turned away the one woman in the world for whom had genuine and abiding feeling. He really had managed to make an awful mess of his life and had entangled both Judith and Anna in that mess.

For the second time that week Nigel wept.

13

(Evia, Greece)

Anna looked at the clock. It was worse than she had feared, she was already late for work, and grabbing her big handbag she dashed out of the house without even switching off the computer. OK the car keys should be in her handbag, but where the hell were they? That is where she usually kept them but they were just not there. A feverish second search of the whole bag proved just as fruitless. Perhaps the damn things were in the house. What an incompetent idiot she was. They were not on her desk, surely that is where she last had them, but there was no trace. With a rising sense of panic she dashed from room to room, piece of furniture to piece of furniture. Bloody hell keys don't just disappear on their own, what on earth had she done with them, they had to be in the house somewhere. Think, woman, think. She must have had them in her hands just before she received that email from Nigel which had been responsible for sending her mind flying up into the clouds.

More precious minutes flew by, she would now be so late getting to school – if she ever managed to get there at all. She must stay calm, it was the only way to find these keys. In a collected manner she carefully went from room to room, searching in all the most unlikely places. No, there was no sign of them in the bedroom so, there was only the bathroom left. Then she would be getting really desperate. And there the blasted things were, languidly resting just below the mirror on the shelf where she kept her basic cosmetics. Of course! She had rushed into the bathroom to check once more on her hair and put on some lipstick so that she could take that photo of herself to send to Nigel.

Keys in hand she rushed back to the car, setting off at high speed to gain every minute that she could. At last Nigel now had a face and physical presence that allowed her to think of him as a real person. Surely he should not be invading her mind now, whilst she was in such a rush? She enjoyed thinking of his image; it was so much better than the idealized image of the man that had increasingly invaded her thoughts with each passing day. Oh, that last message of his, she could feel the intensity of the longing and desire. She teased out each word he had written for further meaning and implication. And he was indeed coming to see her, responding so quickly that he must have wanted exactly the same thing, even before she had mentioned it. A part of him, either consciously or not, was not only ready for that meeting but must have anticipated the inevitability of it.

An overwhelming wave of contentment and happiness swept away all the anxiety about her lateness for work. She just did not give a damn about it. The day that had started rather dim and cloudy suddenly appeared brighter and warmer. The fields were greener, the flowers as colourful as ever and the air so fragrant. She tuned into some music and sang along with the happy love song that was serendipitously playing on the radio. All earlier doubt, fears, and reserve now disappeared, cancelled and wiped out by the assurance of that happy news from Nigel, and by the anticipation and the joy that it brought. The world, her world, seemed like a better place this morning. She was becoming besotted and she knew it, but she was totally incapable of resisting it and she didn't even want to. When was the last time she had felt like this? She had no idea, it was just too far back in her past.

The school bell had sounded long ago and lessons had already started before she arrived. Apart from the students that she was due to teach for the first period all the pupils had disappeared into their allotted classrooms. Her children showed obvious signs of disappointment on seeing her arrive, no doubt hoping for an idle fun hour. But in striking contrast with the previous days the lesson went smoothly and was quite satisfying. The children seemed more eager to listen to her and she had been more imaginative in capturing their attention and interest. The hour, well what was left of it, was over before she even knew it. This was a really good day at work and she would have felt quite hopeful about her future at the school had it not been for that note from the Principal saying that he wanted to see her in his office at first break. This was unlikely to be a pleasant interview.

"Mrs. Dimitriou" the Principal started in an austere, clear and loud voice as soon as she had managed to stutter an apology for her lateness. His manner extinguished any hope of her accomplishing her first good day at work without it being spoiled. "I am sure you know that you were appointed to this post as a replacement of Mrs. Stavrakou, who has taken maternity leave. And although she is expected to resume her responsibilities in the next academic year in our school, you Mrs. Dimitriou, could perhaps get another post during that year, at another school in the area. I hope you realise, that you are being evaluated on your achievement throughout this academic year. Such evaluation includes professionalism and other virtues such as punctuality and respect for the school's rules. I will overlook your lateness on this occasion, as this is the first time, but bear in mind that should this transgression be repeated, it will show up in my report on you".

Anna could feel her blood boiling. She could feel it rushing up her face, pressing her temples, making her feel exceedingly hot. This man had not shown the slightest interest in the efficacy of her teaching and she doubted he had any idea or cared but one jot about how well she did in her teaching. All he was interested in was how things looked, how to keep the flock in the stockyard, regardless of how well they were doing academically within their classes of if they were bone idle.

She did not pause to consider what she was doing. Suddenly she was blurting out things that were foolish in the extreme, things that she should have kept to herself and which, in their saying, were as good as subscribing her to the long-term unemployment list.

"Mr. Konstantinou, I understand your concern and you are quite right. I'm very sorry. But I think it would be a lot more useful if you showed equal concern for the actual functioning of this school and the quality of the lessons provided for the students.

I cannot say I have noticed such concern from you to date. I imagine that you're aware that the school lacks even the most basic equipment for the conduct of lessons such as mine, so you must also understand that this turns my every lesson into a very sick sort of joke".

It was the Principal's turn to flush this time. She had certainly taken him aback but before he opened his mouth to respond to this attack, Anna added, "You may report on me as you wish, sir, and now if you don't mind, I have a class to teach." She turned to leave before Mr. Konstantinou had managed to regain his composure.

So that was it as far as her teaching career was concerned, yet she could not really care less. This was no place for her, she had felt it right from her first moment here. She would never have managed to put up with all the pretence for much longer, even if she had wanted to. She pushed to the back of her mind the threatening prospect of starvation now that this promising source of income had been eliminated. She would just have to see what life had in store for her.

Nigel's image flashed again into her mind, as unexpected as it had been earlier. It soothed her, as if the calmness of his nature, his tranquillity, was flowing into her from afar. She embraced that feeling and kept him close as she stepped into the next classroom, indeed into the rest of the lessons she had for the day. In spite of the unpleasant conversation with the Principal, her good mood had been very quickly restored and she got through her lessons with considerable success – if such term was relevant under the circumstances. The main thing was that she had not suffered much.

She had driven to school fast, now she drove back home at almost the same speed. Would Nigel have replied? That reply of hers regarding his suggestion that they should sleep together was worrying her. Might he have perceived that as a rejection on her part? No, he shouldn't have, she had made that clear. Nigel had always been so quick in understanding her, sometimes responding in the exact manner she needed him to, although she might not have even realised that herself at the time. Could he have misunderstood her now? Oh, don't be silly Anna. She tried to put herself together as a grave feeling of anxiety started to well up within her.

She parked her car and was surprised to see that her hand was not all steady as she tried to put the key in the front door lock. She managed to refrain from sitting in front of her computer as soon as soon as she went into the hose. She had to have some lunch first, although she this was just prolonging her anxious anticipation in an almost masochistic fashion. She ate the food with a total lack of interest, just another task that had to be completed. She lit up a cigarette then sat in front of her screen. It was a good thing that she had left the computer switched on. She really appreciated the precious moments that it had saved her by doing so. She clicked on 'Connect' and then refreshed her Inbox, and there it was; new message, with 'Nigel Marston' glowing against the 'sender' side. A name that was as a poem to her.

She opened the email. As she read through the lines, as one word led her to the next, her joy and her hope and everything good that she had felt that very morning just withered. Her soul shrivelled under the weight of that rejection. By the time she got to the end of his short message, she could hear the sound of her heart cracking. She looked at the message in disbelief. Who was this stranger writing to her under the name of Nigel? She read it again, and it was not before she had completed reading it for the fourth time in a row that she was fully convinced that she had made no mistake.

Not only Nigel had withdrawn from her, not only had he used the cold tone and the language of a total stranger, not only was he more or less telling her that he regretted they had gone as far as they had, but he was actually clearing himself of any responsibility for their actions by putting the onus on her parents and the Greek way of life.

Oh, the surprise, no the shock, to see how insensitive, how egotistical this man she thought she loved could be once his precious placidity and his convenience were threatened. She was so stupid, so incredibly ridiculous. She wanted to slap herself to drive out those images of herself driving happily, singing love-songs like some stupid teenage girl. The shame of it. She was 40 years old and should have known better than to follow her heart. How could she have trusted him so quickly, how could she have allowed herself to surrender emotionally to this total stranger? How on earth had she done so after all that she had been through?

Her eyes started filling with tears of sorrow and rage and disgust. Who did she blame the most? Probably it was herself that she was railing against. It was the naïve, stupid little Anna who had been all too eager to be fooled, and manipulated and used once more. At least with Panos she could be excused, for she had spent half of her life with him, it was at least reasonable that she had believed him, he had after all been her husband, that bastard.

But what about Nigel? What in the world could justify her idiocy in thinking that they could communicate at the level of their souls? That she had found someone in whom she could confide in without causing roars of laughter? She heard the sound of her own laughter, a clear, loud, roaring laughter that was interspersed with equally loud sobbing. Great, she was acting like a lunatic now. She had to bring herself round; this was real life and Nigel a real bastard. And she had been, a real idiot. She hereby forbade herself to cry or to laugh any more.

She went to the bathroom and again she let the downpour of the shower wash away her misery. She stayed long, her soul empty now, with a cavernous space within her chest, and a great gaping hole in place of her heart.

She got out of the shower when the warm water turned cold; well to be more precise when the water had become so cold that it took her breath away. She dried herself meticulously. She combed her hair and brushed her teeth. She put on clean clothes. She made some coffee. She took the mug of coffee and sat at her computer. She looked at the screen and fought hard against the tears that threatened to well up unbidden. Perhaps she had better not answer the email? If she were to be faithful to her nature and her ideals, she should not do so. But she decided that she had had enough of silence and tolerance already today. She wrote:

> *Nigel,*
> *I should say that I am sorry about what happened to*
> *your wife, and to a certain extent, I am indeed. But I*

have more urgent matters to deal with right now. Each of us has their own problems, right?

I will not take up your time or mine, in telling you how this message of yours made feel. I think that is in any case irrelevant. You are, after all we have been through, still a stranger to me, and I am a stranger to you. It doesn't matter if I understand or not, or indeed what it is that I understand. You seem to have it all sorted out.

I hope that your wife makes a quick, full recovery. And I hope that once you have read this message you forget you have ever known me. For this is exactly what you must do.

Anna

No spell check, no proof-reading. She hit the send button just before an indication "connect with another source of energy supply!" flashed on the lower right part of her screen. She stayed, staring blankly at her Inbox page at all those messages, one after another with 'Nigel Marston' as the 'Sender', filled up her screen until it went black. The computer had run out of battery and she had run out of feelings. She closed the lid, put the computer away and went to bed.

(Lake District, UK)

There was an ominous silence. The Land Rover would hardly have been the right vehicle for this fraught task and Nigel had therefor elected to collect Judith in the BMW. German car manufacturers were not high on his list of good charitable organizations, but sadly this X1 ticked all the boxes that other vehicles could not tick. It was supreme in so doing. It was a smug, self-satisfied, robot of a car. He longed for his old Alfa with all its quirkiness and its character.

The hospital had been quietly efficient in dispensing Judith just after teatime into spousal care. A signature here, a sedative there and they were walking together out through the impersonal entrance lobby and across the car park.

"How are you feeling now?"

Silence

"They will have looked after you well enough?"

"I need a drink."

"I asked Clapton to get on with doing something about that step, sorry about not getting it sorted earlier, I daresay the fall was my fault."

"I need a bloody drink."

It dawned upon Nigel that his wife was not in the least distracted by what had happened to her. He glanced at this familiar woman sitting beside him, a stranger in all but name. Her features were fixed as of stone and her eyes were focused into the far distance. He had no idea what he ought to do, how to remedy the situation. He had little doubt that this was his reward for his internet infidelity rather than just another 'bad moment' that Judith was experiencing.

The journey home was swift, but hardly restful.

"Look, we need to talk," he said once they were both in the sitting room holding cups of Lady Grey. "You read those e-mails between Anna and myself, and I admit that I went too far. I'm sorry. I will look after you as I should."

"No you bloody well won't!"

What the hell did she mean by that? Presumably 'won't look after me'. Well at least she was speaking to him, even if 'co-operative' was hardly the name of the game. He drew in a deep breath and slowly exhaled. "I said I that I would and I won't let you down."

"You say a lot of things; few of them true. You are a liar and a cheat. You have let me down and cheated on me."

"Well I mean it, I really do. I will look after you. I've written to Anna and told her that I have a duty and a responsibility to my wife that I cannot and will not gainsay. I'm sorry, because I know that in doing so I will have really hurt Anna"

"Bugger Anna."

There did not appear to be a high degree of intellectual content to this retort, nor did there seem to be a great meeting of minds. Nigel carefully placed his teacup on the tray. He opened his mouth with the intention of trying to explain to his wife that the relationship with Anna was over.

"I'll get changed. I'm going out."

"Out? Out where?"

"None of your bloody business, you apology for a husband." With that Judith, with head held high and her face presenting to the world in general a living picture of the 'wronged wife', walked slowly from the room leaving Nigel speechless. Where the hell was she going?

An hour later Nigel had composed an e-mail to Anna. It was hardly an apology, or even an explanation. He just wanted her to know how he was feeling.

My Dearest Anna,

I realize that I have hurt you deeply. That I most certainly did not intend to do, and would not have wished to do for all the world. I doubt if anything that I say is going to make me appear, in your eyes, to be anything other than an untrustworthy rat, and I quite understand that you may never want to hear from me again. I can only say that you have misunderstood me, and to terrible effect.

I have within me a great compulsion to write to you. I do not mean that I have something specific to write to you about. But I have within me such feeling for you that I am compelled to write. I doubt if that will move you to write back to me. I am unable to control this feeling inside me. I cannot speak to you of 'hurt' as that is something that I know you are feeling with a vengeance, but my heart hurts also. Anna, I know that my feeling for you is oh so real.

With the most affectionate wishes,
Your desolate, Nigel

Without much hope and with no expectation whatsoever, Nigel sent the note. As he was doing so there was a ring at the front door. Another followed and Nigel remembered that Zenca was not working at the house today. He opened the door.

"Taxi for Mrs. Marston.

"What? I don't know anything about this."

"Ordered just an hour ago, sir."

"For the hospital?" asked Nigel, but before the driver could reply Judith swept passed out of the house. The smell of over-applied perfume hit Nigel full in his nostrils. His wife was dressed for the kill. She wore high-heeled shoes, a dangerously low-cut dress, over-applied make-up, an excess of jewellery. The effect was overpowering but somehow she had avoided looking like an old woman dressed to impress a younger audience, indeed the overall impression was that of a very sophisticated tart. It might well be that this was the image that she wished to portray.

Nigel put out his hand to stop her, but she was already getting into the taxi and the driver had started the engine.

"Hey." He felt foolish, "Where are you going?"

The car moved smoothly away and Judith deigned to look at him. She smiled sweetly. Nigel scowled, turned and went indoors.

The deep gloom in his psyche became tinged with a cool anger. His actions, his life, his emotions were being played with, corrupted even. He was being turned this way and that, a weathercock in a changing breeze. Was he Judith's protector or was he just her provider? Was he the love of Anna's life or was he something repugnant to her? He paced the room. He went out into the garden and mooched moodily around the lawn. He surveyed the mess that had been made of his rose bed by Judith's efforts at pond making. He sat unhappily upon a canvas chair on the terrace and looked towards the high fells. There, surely, he would find an answer.

But no answer came.

A little stiffly he returned to the den and his computer

My Darling Anna,

I well know that I am not your 'Darling Nigel', but that must be as it is. I feel my heart reaching out to you across the distance between us. I am not asking to be forgiven for what I said. I stand by that. But it is unforgivable that in making my point you have misunderstood me and so I have hurt you. I know you for the real person that you are – how much I would prefer to be able to say that I know you for the real flesh and blood person that you are. Words can mean so little when we do not look into each other's eyes and confirm the truth of that which we are saying.

I am floundering in a wilderness. My mind knows little except deep despair – the despair of losing contact with the only person with whom I have felt a kinship of such intensity as I have felt with you.

I do not expect a reply. I do not deserve a reply. I can only hope that you will bring yourself to a point where you are able to read what I write to you without feeling the deepest disgust for me.
With the deepest affection,
Nigel

She wouldn't write, he knew that in his heart. But there was within him a hollowness that needed filling, and he was also aware, as he sent the e-mail, that he had no option, he was committed to this one-sided communication with his Greek love.

It was nearly midnight when there was the sound of car wheels upon gravel. A few moments later Nigel heard the clatter of the front door being flung open and the cries of revellers in his hallway. There appeared to be several people and Nigel could hear Judith's voice quite plainly "In here boys, this is where we can have such fun."

He hesitated. This was pay-back time for him and his peccadilloes. Judith was a capable flirt and she had always enjoyed the company of men, preferably groups of men – perhaps there was some safety in numbers in flirting with more than one. But this was different. There was real purpose here. He had to intervene. He opened the door of the den and walked into the sitting room.

There were three men, much of an age, around 30-ish and a younger woman. The CD player had been turned on and Judith was smooching with two of the men at the same time, displaying more leg than was either seemly or safe.

"Darlings," exclaimed his wife, "look who is here, meet my cuckold!" Faces turned towards Nigel. Mocking faces, leering faces, lustful faces. He turned to leave.

"Don't leave, darling, come and watch. It's not every day that you can obtain a grandstand view of yourself being cuckolded!"

The sandy-haired man and the girl started to giggle. He said something to her, looking at Nigel, and she burst out laughing.

"Who the hell are you?" he said "get out of my house – now!"

"Come on, darling Nigel, these are my guests, my very welcome guests, aren't you boys." Judith, one arm around each of the men with her and gave their buttocks a playful squeeze.

Nigel stooped to pick up the poker from the fireplace. His face was pale, he was sweating, he growled "Bugger Off". No one moved. "Fuck off, all of you now!" He advanced upon Sandy-Man and Giggler. He raised the poker.

"Come on Phyllis, we're out of here." As the couple scrambled to their feet the other two men started towards the door, taking Judith along with them. 'Boys, where are you going, what are we going to do?"

Nigel fancied he heard just a tinge of alarm in Judith's voice but he was beyond caring. He wanted them out, all of them out, especially his so-called wife – out. The door slammed behind the departing oafs and Nigel retreated once more to the den.

After ten minutes he picked up his pen and started to assemble words. Much later he turned to the computer keyboard:

> *My Darling Anna,*
>
> *I need to say so many things to you, but I am tongue-tied. I simply cannot say what I want to in prose, indeed I am not sure how to say it by any other means, but our relationship started through poetry and my heartfelt hope is that it can be re-kindled through the same medium. I have written a sonnet, a sonnet to you. As you will gather it is about the power of Love, and I am attaching it to this e-mail.*
>
> *Judith has made it abundantly clear by her actions of this evening that she does not need me. All I can, and need, to do*

now is to make sure she is properly provided for financially and that she receives the care that she will, in future, require. It is more than likely that we will get divorced, although should she object to that I would settle for a legal separation.

What I would love, Anna, is for us to give this extraordinary relationship of ours another chance. Not an Internet chance, but a real physical chance. The choice is yours. If you wish to continue in your rejection of me you will have broken my heart, but I will have no alternative but to accept the situation. If on the other hand you can see just a chink of a possibility for us then do please write to me in the hope that we can arrange to meet each other in Greece.

I long to hear back from you
Your very affectionate
Nigel

Perhaps there was hope. He did not know. He knew that this was the last throw of the dice and it was with the fatalism of an experienced gambler that Nigel hit the Send button on his iMac.

The phone call came at precisely nine thirty the following morning. It was expected and pretty well dead on time, just the location was uncertain. Was he Mr. Nigel Marston?

"Yes, speaking."

"I have been asked by your wife to let you know that she is here with us at The Royal Hotel and she would very much like you to come over and collect her."

"Is she OK?"

"I really couldn't say." The receptionist either did not know or did not want to give too much information away.

There was a certain sense of deja vu about the drive, but whilst the collection of an injured wife from hospital undoubtedly calls for deployment of a saloon car, the recovery of same, but errant, wife from a nearby hotel is more of a Land Rover job. What on earth was he to expect from this message. Well at least the Royal was not too bad as far as Lake District hotels go There were far worse places than this within the immediate area that she might have ended up sleeping it off. It was a mild relief that she had found a bed for the night.

Hello, my name is Nigel Marston, I've come to collect my wife. Is she still in her room?

"I think so."

"Good, perhaps you could let me have the number and I'll go up and fetch her. No need for anyone to show me the way."

The girl behind the desk looked a bit embarrassed, perhaps she was worried about saying too much, anything. She seemed to be consulting a database on her computer, but did not hit the keyboard. "One moment, please." She poked her head around the half mirror glass door at the rear of the small reception cubicle and spoke to someone closeted in the inner sanctum. She stood with her back to Nigel, so that he could not make out what was going on. Eventually she turned with a fixed smile on her face, "If you care to wait for just a moment sir. I have arranged for one of our staff to take you to your wife's room." As if to avoid any further exchange of information the girl now turned to her computer and typed furiously upon the keyboard.

A young man appeared wearing a dark blue tee shirt with a white elephant described upon it, and black and white check trousers. He stopped briefly to have a word with the receptionist, then slouched over to Nigel.

"Come with me."

"Hey," said Nigel, a little bemused by this treatment, "where are you taking me?"

"Staff quarters."

They walked out the back of the hotel into a shingled yard. A paved path brought them around a scruffy hedge. In front of them stood a low two-story concrete building that resembled a stark barrack block. The young man shoved open the external door with a practiced shoulder and Nigel followed him in. The place smelled of unwashed socks, cigarettes smoke and something stickily sweet that might have been drugs. The smoking ban seemed somehow irrelevant. Ahead of them lay a flight of uncarpeted stone stairs with an iron bannister. As they went up Nigel asked what Judith was doing in this place. It was possible that his companion did not hear him, but more likely that the words were just ignored. On reaching the top of the stairs they turned to their left and started along a dingy corridor, pushing aside a couple of half-dressed young men. At the third door on the left Nigel's guide stopped He flipped his right hand dismissively at the door. "In there," he said, and retreated whence he had come.

This was not right. What the hell was Judith doing in here in a place like this? There was no doorknob and no catch. He pushed the door open.

Inside the room the tatty yellow curtains were partly drawn filtering the light that might have reached the room despite the massive bank of dark trees that lay behind the place. There were clothes and plastic carrier bags and shoes scattered about on the stained purple carpet.

He walked in squeezing passed the cream-coloured dressing table that was home to a number of dubious objects including a small television set that was burbling garbage to itself.

Judith lay upon the single bed that took up a large part of the room. There was a grubby sheet covering about half of her body, but from that which Nigel could see she appeared to be naked. "Ah, you've come. Good. Enter my parlour, oh my cuckold, you have made good time"

"What the hell are you doing here?" The enormity of what Judith might have been up to drilled itself right into him, exploding in his head, "What are you doing in this stinking cesspit of a room?"

"My darling cuckold, best not to enquire"

Nigel looked at the grubby washstand, the discarded sheets, the body of this woman that was still his wife. They all revolted him. His throat was dry. He wanted to puke. He opened his wallet and took out twenty quid. He placed it on the dressing table. "Get yourself a bloody taxi. I want nothing more to do with you." With that he made for the door.

As he retreated down the corridor one of the two rather scruffy man that he had passed earlier accosted him "Hey, mate, get real. That was my turn, you might have bloody waited for yours." Nigel shrugged him off.

The Land Rover drove itself home, Nigel – a mere passenger. What the hell had happened to the woman that was once his charming wife? The woman he had loved, and trusted. How could she possibly behave in such a manner? There was absolutely no doubt as to what she had been doing. Her companions of yesterday evening must have been hotel staff, and there was she stark bollock naked in a bed that she had clearly shared with several of her new-found 'friends'.

Yes, she had been very drunk, but this was far worse than anything she had ever done before. Perhaps her learning of his loving feelings towards Anna had given her cause for being upset, perhaps very upset, but this was beyond anything he could possibly have imagined.

Nigel sought the comfort of his computer:

My Darling Anna,

I am in a terrible state. Whilst I know that I upset Judith when she discovered that I had such strong feelings for you, I find that I no longer know my wife. She has done things and said things that I cannot bring myself to tell you about in writing, I will talk it all through with Judith as sensibly as we can, but it is the end of our marriage.

Whilst I confess that it is Judith's recent behaviour that has forced my hand and helped resolve our situation, I am now able to say, with clarity and with love that I would like to come and see you, in Greece, as soon as I possibly can. I want us to look each other in the eyes, hold each other by the hand, and be certain that the deep feelings we have expressed to each other over the Internet are indeed real.

I have not heard from you since you said you wanted nothing more to do with me. I understand how you felt, that I had let you down, that I was unprepared to fully commit at that stage, and that this did not show true loyalty. But things have moved on and I cannot believe that you can read what I have been sending to you over the last couple of days and not feel just a twinge of that glorious emotion that you expressed so freely and with such loving strength. I think that you still have feelings for me, and I most certainly have the deepest affection for you that I need to express that by holding you and never letting you go.

Please do not hesitate, my Anna, remember what you said to me about regretting those experiences that you fail to embrace in this life. Do not let me be one of those regrets.

With the deepest affection
Nigel

There was no question of pausing and re-reading what he had written this time. Nigel knew what he wanted. He wanted Anna. He had written clearly and from his heart. If she rejected him now then he would have to take that as her final word.

The sound of the front door opening reached the den. He listened to Judith pulling herself slowly up the stairs and then the sound of the bathroom door closing.

Half an hour later his bathed, and remarkably fresh-looking, wife joined him in the conservatory, wafting in wearing a blue dress and smelling of lavender. She slid onto the smaller of the two chairs, looked up and smiled at him sweetly, "So, my darling, we are quits. We are now even with each other are we not?"

Did she not understand what she had just done? Did she not realize that in her intimacy with the casual hotel staff at the Royal she had behaved in a manner so disgusting that he could no longer live with her? "We need to talk this through sensibly."

"Nigel, what the hell are you talking about?"

"I am talking about divorce."

For a moment Judith seemed taken aback, but she rallied quickly and even managed a small laugh, "You are funny, my sweet. Fancy talking about divorce just because of a tiny bit of infidelity? Don't worry I won't hold it against you any longer. Mind you I don't want you to go on writing to her, I am not that broad-minded."

"It's not me, for Christ's sake, it's you."

"I never said I loved anyone, I never planned to fly away to a foreign country to have a dirty weekend, I never wrote to a lover about my deepest emotions. Oh no, darling, all I did was have a bit of fun fucking with a few of my boys."

"Do you want to go on living here?"

"Of course I do, it suits us perfectly. Why should we move now?"

"I don't mean 'us' I mean 'you', just you by yourself, once we have separated."

It took an hour.

A long, painful, tedious, nerve-wracking hour for Nigel to get it into Judith's head that he was serious about divorcing her. She continued to deny the possibility at first, and when he finally got it through to her that he meant every word that he was saying she rounded on him and accused him of engineering the whole situation so that he had a first-rate excuse to go off and fuck his provocative little Greek floosy.

"She's really got her claws into you, hasn't she? She doesn't want you, my husband, what she wants is your money, your security. No doubt she wants to live in this house of ours."

No amount of explaining would convince Judith that it was her behaviour that had caused this unbridgeable rift between them. She simply made light of it, as if it did not matter in the least. Nor did his saying that he was thinking of joining Anna in Greece disabuse Judith of the absolute certainty that Anna ('that Greek floosy') was angling for him to get her out of a Greece that was disintegrating financially, politically, and now socially.

But he got it through to her in the end. She might not understand, even in her deepest heart, what she had done, but she at last conceded that Nigel was serious.

"Look, "he said, "I want to make sure that you are properly cared for. If you want to go on living here that's fine. We will make the house over to Caroline and Jimmy, with a proviso that you should have it rent-free for as long as you wish to live here. Then you will be entirely secure."

"Oh no. No thanks. A small flat in London will do me fine. I can see my children and have lots of things around to keep me amused." Clearly she was beginning to warm to the idea of being an independent and 'almost single' woman living in London.

"OK, but we will have to work out a proper settlement, then you can have the care that you need."

"Oh bollocks, I don't need any care. All I need, from time to time, is a man to service me. Then I shall be fine."

14

<u>(Evia, Greece)</u>

It was easy to park here at this time of year. In the height of the summer it is well-nigh impossible, especially at the weekends when the Athens crowds descend upon this pretty beach area.

Ellie and Anna were sitting in the taverna overlooking a gorgeous sandy beach dotted with sunshades and loungers. It was cold in the water and Ellie, never the greatest of swimmers, came out long before Anna, who loved swimming. Ever since her early childhood she had felt so at home in the water, especially under the water as she enjoyed diving. Today there were shoals and shoals of multicoloured tiny fish. They look so pretty in this bright spring sunshine and brought a tinge of happiness back into Anna's life.

The waiter brought a bottle of water and two glasses. From the menu Anna chose squid and smoked mackerel. Ellie added gavros and sardines all of which they shared along with a Greek salad. The fish was good here, a specialty of this place. Anna rolled a cigarette and take a long cool pull at it.

"You are still in love with him," said Ellie. It was a statement. There would have been more inflexion in her voice had she not been so certain. Much as she loved speaking English, Anna admitted that sometimes Greek is a more useful language for expression.

"I despise him – for what he has done to me."

"Hate and love, two sides of the same coin."

She was right of course, but it was Trust that had been so wilfully destroyed.

"Trust is so important to me. Some people have trouble in trusting others. I am the opposite. I trust people too much, and I trusted Nigel, allowed him to penetrate my defences in such a way that I have given myself to him absolutely. Once we met there would have been no holding back, no embarrassment, no shame. And now that has all gone. And for what? For some misplaced sense of duty and a miserable soggy wet existence in a far-flung corner of England." She wiped a slightly moist eye.

"But you are right," said Ellie. "You gave all your trust to Panos, and look what happened, he let you down. As soon as you were really his, once he had imprisoned you in marriage and locked you into that 'gilded cage' that you told me about, what did he do? He buggered off and not only shagged another woman, he lived with her, ended up by fathering two kids with her. For goodness sake if that isn't a betrayal of your trust I don't know what is."

"I think he loved me."

"Who, Panos?"

"Yes, well at first he did."

"You are such an innocent, almost as innocent as the day we met, when we were teenagers. Of course he loved you, that is what men are like, they want to own you, they want to possess you – and they call that love. Once they have fucked you they just carry on to the next challenge."

"Not all men."

"True, but certainly Panos."

Anna thought about what her friend was saying, again she was correct. "But I am not sure that applies to Nigel.".

"Perhaps this internet stud of yours is just weak? You say he is in his fifties? Well perhaps he is past it. He is well on his way perhaps to becoming doddery old man?"

They laughed at this and asked the waiter for another beer each.

"He has written to me."

"Nigel?"

"Yes, several times. He even sent me a poem. Quite a good one really, a sonnet that he composed especially for me."

"I am not saying he doesn't have a way with words, but that is hardly the issue."

It was good, seeing Ellie. She waved a cheery goodbye as she dropped Anna off at the end of her road. As the car departed Anna felt a terrible sadness, a very tender sense of loneliness. She had not felt this before she started to write with Nigel, but now she was all too aware that there was something missing from her life. It would take time to again accustom herself to being totally on her own. That seemed so stupid when her 'companion' was two and a half thousand kilometers away and she had never set eyes on him, let alone kissed him, stroked his face, held his body close to hers, or made love to him. But it was how she felt, and feelings were everything to her.

The work at school was getting easier. Strangely the Principal had become quite friendly with Anna, well at least he knew her name and said 'good day' whenever they passed in the corridor. Perhaps no one had ever spoken to him as she had.

Sadly though she was becoming anaesthetised to that feeling of contempt from the Authorities towards teachers and the students too. There was also the dreadful realization that the whole system was collapsing throughout the country, being stifled by the shambles that was now the Greek economic nightmare.

There was good news though. Her newfound friend, the Principal, had agreed to let her have the use of a slide projector so that she could show her students pictures of the great works of art that she had been talking about with them

There was yet another general strike. Anna sat moodily at home. There were only two options that she could see for coping with all those old emails from Nigel. Either erase them or expose them. She decided to opt for the second and so took pains to print out all of them, including the poem. She then and stuck them up on the wall next to the fire. There they hung, like gibbets turning in the breeze as the rising air from the fire caused them to flutter slightly.

She just could not understand the man. Why did he still profess love for her? What could he feel, now that he had so comprehensively destroyed her trust in him? It was a mystery. She wondered if the mind of the male of the species would remain a closed book to her for the rest of her life.

It was such a pleasure when the phone rang and it was her bother calling from France.

"Hi Lukas, how's it going?"

"It's great, little sister, I have a job, not a brilliant one, but at least I am on my way again."

"And the language, how are you managing with it."

"It's cool. Not that difficult. I can make myself understood well enough to place a bet at Longchamps, not that I ever win any-thing. I am sharing a flat with a guy who can speak nearly perfect French. He's American, but don't hold that against him."

She laughed. Lukas well knew that whilst she was something of an Anglophile that did not extend to English-speakers on the other side of the Atlantic. He told her all about Paris and suggested that she should fly up and spend a week with him in the school holidays. She was sorely tempted.

"And how's your love life, little sister, are you still living like a hermit out there in the wilds of Evia?"

"That's a very sore subject just now. I thought I had found someone. Someone very special, but he has let me down."

"How come. Who is he – I'll go round and bash his brains in next time I come home."

"Not much chance of that. He is English. I met him on the internet."

"I see."

"No you don't, you fool. This is, no was, a really good relationship."

She told Lukas all about Nigel and what they had said to each other and how much he had started to mean to her before he totally destroyed her trust in him.

"But what I don't understand," said her brother, "is exactly what he did wrong?"

"Listen," she said, plucking Nigel's 'rejection' email from her wall. She read it out over the phone.

"So?" he said

"What do you mean 'So'? This bloody man just jacked out of my life."

"No he didn't"

They have a brother/sister 'yes he did', 'no he didn't' moment before Lukas started to talk in a serious manner about what he thought Nigel was doing, what he was trying to say to her. Lukas had always been logical, almost the exact opposite of the passionate emotional Anna. He understood how the logical mind worked. He explained that Nigel was planning, he was looking forward, he was trying to cover every eventuality, and as part of that he was trying to protect Anna against the possibility of being let down in a really harsh way.

"Neither of you know whether you would be able to get on with each other. For goodness sake you had never met each other. All he was trying to say is that you should give yourselves a bit more time, and that you should both abandon Cloud Nine and lower your expectations."

He was right of course. Anna felt so stupid. Everyone was always right, except her.

Lukas rang off, repeating his invitation for Anna to go to Paris. He even suggested that she might like to meet Nigel there. The cheek of her young brother!

She started to shake, she clutched the edge of the table and sat rather hastily on one of the chairs. She burst into great racking sobs. She had been such a fool. Such a bloody bloody fool.

It took fifteen minutes for her to overcome her shame and her self-pity sufficiently to allow herself to get out of the chair and walk over to the fireplace wall. With the greatest tenderness she removed each of Nigel's desperate and loving emails, kissing each one in turn and placing it oh so gently into the fire. She had been mocking her best friend, her love, and her soul mate. It must not continue.

Anna went to the computer and stared for a long time at a blank outgoing message page. Then very slowly she started to write.

My Nigel,
What have I done?
What must you think of me?
I have misunderstood your concerns and your worries and
I now realize that they were concerns and worries for me.
How I might feel in the future if things did not turn out
well. Oh, Nigel, we are all at the mercy of events. There
was no need for you to be so protective. I am a free spirit, a
passionate woman. I go with the flow wherever that might

take me. Unlike you I do not plan and worry and torture myself about how the future is going to turn out.
My darling let us make up again, let us indeed take our time, if that is what you want, but do let us be together.
My mind, my heart and my body are crying out to be one with yours.
Your loving Anna
H Avva σου

The message had been sent. She was exhausted. She could take no more. She switched the computer off.

<u>(Lake District, UK)</u>

It is not that he had given up on Anna, far from it. He was fairly certain that she was reading his emails, but feared that she was then either laughing at him or considering him to be an object of pity. He did not enjoy the thought of either scenario. He would have to bottle up his feelings of intense love for this woman, harden his protective shell, and keep his heart to himself.

Nigel wondered if he should get himself a dog. He liked dogs and needed a companion. A canine companion would be good. Dogs do not speak and are only mildly troublesome, which is a whole lot better than humans, particularly female humans, a most particularly female humans that live in Greece.

Then it arrived. Nigel had acquired the habit of only turning the computer on once a day. His spirit had been broken and even the poetry site held little to commend itself to him. So it was early evening before this wonderful email beamed itself into his life. His heart leaped with joy and the dull, rainy darkening day suddenly became a place of colour and light. It was difficult to believe, for he had given up hope. His emotional life had already been slinking back into its deep dark cave and it had been his intention to ensure that it stayed there.

He immediately started to sketch out a reply. But he could not do it. His hands were shaking and his vision was blurred. He had been a poor specimen of a man before Anna's e-mail arrived, now he was a totally helpless wreck.

Oh Anna, I cannot write – I am so full of joy and love and trembles!
O Nigelaki sou

His still shaking hand clicked the mouse over the Send icon and this pathetic little note headed for Greece and for the woman that he loved beyond anything and anyone else in the whole world.

(Evia, Greece)

Anna wanted to switch the computer on again and stay beside it until there was some sort of response from Nigel, however she was objective enough to understand that this would do her no good. She uncorked a new bottle and poured herself a large glass of Pinot Noir. It was getting quite chilly in the evenings now so she pulled on a lightweight fleece and stepped out into the yard.

She sat, gently and slowly sipping her wine and looking out across the olive groves to the shimmering silvery sea in the far distance. She reflected upon how chance and mischance had brought her, both physically to this place, and emotionally to her possibly estranged Englishman. She really hadn't planned for anything like this. Since that shocking phone call and dreadful news of Panos's infidelity – well it was more than mere infidelity, but she did not want to explore that further now – since that time she had hardly made any pre-planned decisions, rather she had just followed her instincts and 'gone with the flow'.

She supposed that this was a personality trait, and not one of which she was particularly proud. When considered from a distance it seemed rather wishy-washy, as if she was incapable of managing her own life. And yet here she was, living in her own cottage, that she had bought with her own money and, at least for now, holding down a job that she had applied for.

Anna shivered slightly, but not from cold. She knew what it was and walked hurriedly to the computer, switching it on and waiting the usual interminable time for it to sort out its connection to the internet.

She read Nigel's crazy note and smiled in genuine amusement and relief. She started to type.

> *My Very Dearest Nigel,*
>
> *It has been so long, too long, to have been away from you. My heart, that had been melting, was already hardening following what I thought was your rejection of me, and now it is melting again, along with the rest of me.*
>
> *For the best part of my life I have followed my heart, not my mind. It landed me in the mess of a loveless marriage, and the strange thing is that I really did not recognize it, even though I was enveloped in it. My heart was telling me that love conquers all, that love is the emotion that makes everything else right and that overcomes all others.*
>
> *Was I wrong? I cannot say, but I am fairly certain that it was not love that let me down. I think it was trust.*

I treasure honesty, and I treasure honesty in you. I see now that it is your honesty that caused you to write as you did, and I took it as a rejection of my trust in you. From such misunderstandings great rifts are born and foul demons are released. I am not sure if the distance between us has affected the way we react with each other over deeply felt emotional issues. I rather doubt it. But perhaps the fact that we started off from totally different points has contributed to it to a certain extent.

What I want to say to you is that we initially came to each other through our minds – mainly as a result of your being a poet, and it is through our minds that we must concentrate on rebuilding this wonderful relationship of ours. All else will surely follow.

But in case you are wondering, I am here for you. Not just in mind and heart, but in body as well, and my body craves the touch of your body.

Your very affectionate
Anna

(Lake District, UK)

Nigel felt calmer now that he had sent that very brief note to Anna. There were things here, at his house, that were crying out for his attention, most particularly getting Judith settled into a flat in London. He was looking to buy somewhere, rather than rent. He intended to put such a place in the joint names of his two children and granting Judith a lease for as long as she should live, at zero rent. He needed to talk to his Chartered Surveyor chum, Matthew about this as he was unsure as to how it could be legally achieved.

He scoured the internet for some considerable time. He was looking to spend no more that 400K and rather surprisingly he found several quite suitable places in his price range. He had thought that London prices might prove too expensive. He would need to discuss this with Judith. The thought of doing so filled him with trepidation. As he got to his feet the computer pinged – and there was a delightful message from Anna. He read it very carefully, then settled down to type a reply.

My darling, my Anna,
You may well be right about it not being distance that matters. Well it does a bit because if we were not so many hundreds of miles apart we would have met each other very early on, and I rather think that you were not then ready for such a meeting? I know that I wasn't. I rather think that being the sort of people that we are has brought us together.
Let us take our journey towards full intimacy at a gentle pace and enjoy the experience in both our minds and our bodies.
I have such a fear of being trapped by circumstance. My marriage was founded upon a lie. Not the overt telling of an untruth, but the more subtle lie of deliberately ceasing to take the Pill, so that the resulting pregnancy led to our marriage. I love my son to bits, but he was the unwitting result of a woman lying to a man. I hope you do not mind my telling you such an intimate thing, but I do not want there to be secrets between us.
We are creative people and because of this we have great imaginations, but we may well be putting upon each other under some considerable emotional strain. Inevitably the

*time will come when we stop being virtual lovers, I hope
and expect that this is through our becoming real and
physical lovers. I think we agree? Whatever the cost is to
ourselves and to our souls, we have no real choice other than
to press on with this glorious adventure of the heart. We
may become frightened at times, or you may be put off by
the way I behave, but if we support each other, if we treat
each other kindly and with respect, then we will achieve an
understanding of trust and of love that I think both of us
have been so deprived of throughout our lives.*

*My darling, we will get to meet, and before long, but as I
said before, let us savour the journey towards that meeting*

*I love you very much, I think of you constantly. You have
bewitched me!*

Nigel

(Evia, Greece)

The phone was ringing and Anna dashed to try to catch it.
In doing so her elbow caught the edge of a light curtain that she
had pulled across the window to keep out the direct sunlight. The
curtain pulled awkwardly behind her bringing with it the curtain
rod and the other curtain with a great crash. Anna tripped and went
sprawling across the floor on her front.

Slightly dazed she pushed herself to her elbows. She took a
quick inventory of her legs arms and head and confirmed that all
were in working order. The phone stopped ringing. To her surprise
the curtains were not damaged at all and the rod had just jumped
out of its hook. It was the work of a couple of minutes to restore
order to her room.

Anna thought the call could only have been from her mother or from Ellie. She did a ring back and was pleased to hear Ellie's voice at the other end.

"Hi, pretty thing," said Ellie, "what have you been up to that stops you from answering my call?"

"Sorry, beautiful girl" said Anna, "I was rushing to answer it but instead of getting to the phone I had an argument with my curtains."

"Curtains usually win arguments."

"Yes, indeed. But no damage done and I have put them back where they belong and given them a strict telling off."

She told Ellie that things were now going well with Nigel, and although she was really desperate to meet this man that was having such an influence on her life, she was also slightly fearful. She also told her about her conversation with Lukas and her subsequent e-mails with Nigel.

"Okay, good, so you are going to meet the guy."

"Yes, but I am a little apprehensive about it."

"Of course you are, but it really is no good just writing gooey e-mails to each other. You need to meet. But what then?"

"What do you mean?"

"Let's assume that you meet, you are not put off by him, you have a few days together, including sex of course, and he then jumps on a plane and returns to England."

"Okay, so what?"

"Exactly! You cannot marry him. You cannot even live with him here in Greece or your mother would make your life miserable, and goodness knows what might happen to your father."

"But I don't really want to live in England with Nigel."

"And you tell me that it could take 18 months or more for him to sort out his various affairs in England – and get his divorce."

"True, and you are of course quite right. But I find it so difficult to think logically and plan, it's just not the sort of person that I am."

Ellie knew this of Anna, but she was worried about her friend and felt that she had to try to get just a little common sense into this wayward relationship. "Stay in touch, my love, and even if logical thinking is not your thing perhaps you could try to get Nigel to think in those terms." She rang off.

Anna tried hard to concentrate on the awkward matters that her friend had raised, but she was no planner, and by default she 'decided' to let things drift. More importantly she needed to reply to Nigel's loving e-mail.

My Very Dearest Nigel,
You exert such an influence over my mind – and I love it. I don't think I have told you much about my friend Ellie? Well I had an interesting conversation with her a few weeks ago about the sort of man that I should 'look for', and it became clear that whilst I am a fully functioning sexual being (I thought you would be pleased to hear that!) it is something much deeper than mere physical pleasure (mere? It's better than that!) which I am so much in need of. It is the mental and emotional stimulation that I am gaining at last, almost for the first time in my life – certainly at this intensity, and that is through you, Nigel.
I have recently had a phone conversation with Ellie, and she is, rightly, concerned as to where this relationship of ours is leading us. Not physically, or even emotionally, but in a practical sense. Where are we going to live. What are we going to live on? Are we intending to get married – with all the legislative and financial consequences.

Nigel my dear, I cannot really think about all this, let alone come up with answers, but before long we will might well have to.

I am so pleased, no not just pleased, but humbled, that you told me about the lie that entrapped you into your first marriage. It is an awful thing to live with and I just want to hold you to me and comfort you. I want you to know that you can have absolute trust in me and that I would never break that trust, and certainly not in such a cruel and cynical way, and you can be certain that I will never 'trap' you into anything. We are free spirits and we are entering this relationship of our own will, unencumbered by guilt or responsibility.

From you, my dearest, I do not want money, I do not want lifestyle, what I desire is you. Yes, the whole of you, mind, body and spirit. I can only offer me – but I do so with an openness and a complete denial of self – Nigel I am yours, take me to heaven, take me any way you wish for I love you.

Anna sou

(Lake District, UK)

Judith was sitting in the conservatory, looking relaxed, indeed almost happy, and sipping a mug of coffee. Nigel wandered in holding a sheaf of photocopies and sat half-opposite her, the glass-topped table between them. "How are you feeling?" he said.

There was no reply. He put the printouts on the table and spread them out. "I have been looking for a suitable flat in central London for you to live in. I was quite surprised to find a number of quite decent ones in our price range.'

"Why should I want to live in London"

Nigel patiently explained that they had been through all that several times already and that it was part of their arrangements for divorce.

"But I don't want to live in London. I hardly know the place, and certainly have no friends there."

"Where do you want to live ten?"

"I want us to stay here, my dear old cuckold."

Nigel ignored the sobriquet and explained, yet again, that they had to sell this house so that once they were divorced they could each afford a place of their own.

"Well, just give me the money, I can deal with the whole thing."

"Its not like that. As we have discussed your flat will be owned jointly by Jimmy and Caro. You will have a lease for life at zero rent."

"That's gross. So you and your floozie can buy your own house anywhere you like, England or Greece, and yet you shackle me to live in rented accommodation."

To Nigel fairness was everything and this accusation struck at his very heart. In a cool, detached way he explained that his new home would also be owned by their two children, and he would have a similar arrangement to hers regarding his tenure of the place.

"Well whatever you say, my cuckold," and she started to shout, "I am not going to live in London. Why the hell should I?" So saying with great force she slammed her coffee mug down on the table. With a great crash the table top broke into a hundred slivers of glass."

"Blast you." Said Nigel, taking the mug from her.

"Never mind Nigel, dear. You just got a bit excited. It will clear up, and you can buy us another table."

Zenca, as usual, came swiftly into the room at the sound of breakage and moved to help Judith get up and walk towards the sitting room.

"I am so sorry Zenca, my idiot husband has had a tiny accident with the coffee table," said Judith, "he does this sort of thing sometimes, it really is very silly of him. I keep telling him that he ought to behave."

Zenca looked at Nigel, who shrugged and turned away. He started picking up shards of glass and putting them on last week's copy of Horse and Hound.

"Leave that to me, Mr. Marston, we don't want you bleeding all over the place."

Nigel thanked Zenca, ignored his wife, and made his way to his study. He read Anna's loving message to him, and set about composing a reply.

> *My darling Love, my Anna,*
> *Your last email raised a lot of things that interest and intrigues me.*
> *I have found someone with whom I can interact, a complex and very real and fascinating person. In short you, Anna. And it is you that I want to be friends with, to be in love with and, if you want it as well, to make love with.*
> *I know that there is something more important than mere self-gratification about our meeting. Incidentally I think we are both now agreed that this is definitely going ahead? Mind you if you change your mind, then that is your prerogative.*
> *With my deepest affection*
> *Your Nigel*

(Evia, Greece)

Anna was bustling about tidying the house up. She had really neglected housework recently, being too upset to think about it. Now she whizzed around with duster and Hoover, polishing and wiping down until the place began to look decent again. She was however within hearing distance of her computer, and when it pinged she was able to read Nigel's message straight away.

She thought of all the things that she wanted to tell Nigel, but decided that almost all could wait until they met. Just the thought of their meeting set her tingling inside. His email demanded a swift response.

> *My darling, my Nigel,*
> *Sometimes it seems to me that I can read your thoughts, I can 'feel' it when you think of me. I don't know how I know these things, my love. I guess that for the main part of my life I've always been somewhat "sensitive", I have never, ever, experienced anything like this with anybody in my whole life. I have not been like this for anybody. I'm equally confused because I can't rationally explain the way I feel for you.*
> *You are an absolutely wonderful man, and though not flawless (who is?), you are everything I have ever wished for.*
> *Your passionate.*
> *Anna*

(Lake District, UK)

This could not go on! Nigel yearned for some sort of resolution, and this could only be achieved by his travelling to Greece, meeting, and staying with, Anna. It was time to make plans, at least short-term ones. He thought carefully, consulted his diary, had a quick word with Zenca to see how available she might be next week to look after Judith, then sat down to write to Anna

My darling, my Anna,

So how would you feel about my coming to see you in Greece for, say, four days next week? I am suggesting that as being long enough to know that we really are right for each other – and not so long that in the very unlikely event of our not getting on it will seem like an eternity!

Should we go to your place, or to a small hotel? I will leave it entirely up to you. We need a quiet time where we can swim, lie in the sun, drink good wine, make love and just feel our way into each other's lives. Does this sound good to you? I could fly out on Wednesday, returning on Sunday. Will you meet me at the airport?

We will need to discuss what happens after this meeting. Let us assume that everything that we have both dreamed of actually happens and we discover that this close emotional bond is our reality. Then what happens next? Do I come to live with you in Greece? Do you come to England. Would either of us be happy, long term, in a foreign country. I cannot answer that. I think we just have to feel our way and all will be well.

So it really is going to happen? Oh, Anna, I am starting to tremble again at the very thought of it. I want so much to be with you, to look into your eyes, and to say to you all the things that we have written about.

Your very own
Nigel

(Evia, Greece)

He's coming, he's coming, he's coming! Anna was beside herself with excitement. She phoned Ellie, but got no answer, she phoned Lukas and got his answering machine, upon which she left no message. She would have loved to have phoned her mother, but sadly that was out of the question. For the moment at least Nigel's presence in Greece had to be kept from her mother. She sat down and thought about the practicalities involved and made a few phone calls.

A little later she wrote to Nigel.

> *My Very Dearest Nigel,*
>
> *Well I have been working very hard on your 'practical' side of things, although I freely confess that such matters do not exactly stir my soul! I thought seriously about us driving back here to my home. It is a place where we could sort of try out life together. I could cook for you, we could swim, and we could relax. However I think that for this first meeting we might do better on 'neutral' territory, it would be less of a commitment. There is a lovely little place on the far coast of Evia, and I can book an apartment for us there.*
>
> *You are right about the future. We don't know yet if there will be one, and if there is we cannot plan for it, we must, as you say, just feel our way. But we will find a way!*
>
> *Of course I will meet you at the airport. I cannot wait until I see you emerging from the airside exit into the Arrivals Hall – oh what a moment that will be!*
>
> *Until Wednesday next - I am waiting for you . . .*
> *Your Anna*

(Lake District, UK)

It was at very short notice that Jimmy and Caroline had turned up at the family home. Jimmy had picked his sister up in Leeds, where she had been working, and they had made their way north-west in his Range Rover.

They had been greeted by Nigel, and all three of them had gone through to the sitting room to find Judith. There was a great hugging and exclamations of joy and Judith was clearly delighted to see them. Zenca brought in some tea and cake.

Jimmy, as usual, took the bull by the horns. "So you are heading fairly rapidly for divorce?"

Judith looked at him blankly, "who is? A friend of yours?"

Caroline took her by the hand, "no Mum, Jim is talking about you and Nige. We came up to see you both to talk about it, and where you are both going to live."

Judith looked at her daughter in some amazement. "Caro dear, I don't understand. Your father and I are fine. He has had a little flirtation, but men will be men (particularly at his age) and I have forgiven him for it."

Jimmy turned towards Nigel, "But, Nige, you said that the two of you had worked things out and that Mum was happy to take a flat in London."

"That's how it was," said Nigel, "but your mother tends now to have a very selective memory. We agreed on a two year 'no fault' divorce, but I am wondering if that timescale is unrealistic. We could go for adultery."

"Ah, your little Greek floosy," said Judith, "but I have forgiven you for that."

Caroline looked a bit confused. She turned to Nigel, "Perhaps you meant that Mum was the adulterer?"

"Caro!" Said Judith, "what an awful thing to say about your mother. What has your father been telling you behind my back?"

"Mum, your behaviour at The Royal was really appalling, more than enough to give Nige grounds for divorce by adultery."

"Tush" said Judith, "I was just playing games with my boys." And with that she flounced out of the room and headed for the stairs.

Nigel looked at his two children, "I am afraid that all this is having a rotten effect on the two of you."

"And you Nige," said Caroline, "but what exactly is going on between you and this woman in Greece?"

Nigel explained the situation. That he and Anna had not yet met, but were proposing to meet in a few days' time. He told them how he had tried to support Judith, who undoubtedly was ill, but that awful business in the staff quarters of the hotel was more than he could take.

"Will you marry this Anna?" asked Jimmy

"I really don't know. We have certainly not made any plans yet, indeed we haven't even decided to live together. I just hope that the two of you are okay about this?"

"Our main concern is about Mum," said Jimmy. The way things are going she may well end up in a care home. Do you have the funds for that?"

"Once this house is sold and two small places bought, that is a flat in London, and a cottage in this sort of area, then there most certainly will be enough for Judith's care for a good long time."

Jimmy and Caroline had left by six o'clock. Nigel was worried about them, but pleased that they had made the time to come and discuss things, and also get a taste of Judith's difficult behaviour. Rather reluctantly he climbed the stairs in search of his wife. Judith was nowhere to be found.

"Zenca, have you seen Mrs. Marston recently"

"Oh yes, she went out. She told me she was taking the BMW and could I let you know not to wait up for her."

15

(Manchester Airport, UK, 6 days later)

Anna My darling
Just about to board the plane. Had to get up at 3.30 to get
here and clear security. Weather is OK, looks as if we should be
on time. I want you so much and am longing to hold you in
my arms
Nigel

(On plane, taxying. Manchester airport)

A
Capt. said arr 15 mins early
N

(Eleftherios Venizelos airport, Greece.)

My Nigel,
I know you cannot receive this until you land – but I will be at the
Arrivals, waiting for you with oh so much longing. I can hardly
contain myself.
Your Anna

Darling Nigel,
I am waiting – the arrivals board says your plane has just landed
Your Anna

The γαμημένος plane landed ages ago. Anna saw it marked as such on the Arrivals board. Where the devil is he? Surely he would have managed to get a message to her if he missed the flight? There are people trickling out of the exit towards this small expectant crowd. He is not amongst them. She stands to one side, partly to get a better view, but also because she hates crowds. She wants him to see her alone. She has been alone for such a long time.

A – landed – with you soon. N

She sees the hat first. Only an Englishman of a certain type would get away with wearing a hat like that. He is almost exactly as she has pictured him from his photos, with his hair just as grey as she thought it would be. He is wearing a sort of white safari jerkin and long trousers. He will be hot. He doesn't understand Greece in the summer. Poor Nigel!

Nigel sees her. She is standing quite alone in this crowded place, wearing a blue dress, cornflower blue with a halter neck and flared at the waist. It is her eyes that capture him. A blue-grey gaze that is so intense that it wants to reach inside him and tear hungrily into his heart. His legs are curiously reluctant to carry him those final steps through from the non-Schengen exit barrier into the main Arrivals Hall, and to Anna.

They stare at each other. There have been photos, but this is the real thing. At last, after all those e-mails they are experiencing each other's presence for the first time. She is so real. Her hair is lighter than Nigel had expected and even in this neon-lit airport there is a golden sheen to it, a head of curls caressed by an ancient sun. She is so pretty. He knew she would be. And she wears no make-up, none at all. It gives her an honest, truthful air. He moves towards her and, as he reaches her, she tilts her head up towards him.

Anna lets him, Nigel, come to her. It is what she craves, a man who wants her, who will keep on coming to her, again and again, who puts his arms around her and pulls her to him, just as he does now. She feels the vibrancy in his body. It is much more powerful that she could ever have expected and she tilts her head slightly so that he can bend to kiss her. His lips part and without a second thought she pushes her tongue into his mouth. They already know each other so well. Introductions would be intrusive.

The End

or perchance . . .

I would like to thank those who helped the creation of this book, unflinchingly steering me in the right direction, nullifying most of my peccadilloes, suggesting revisions to the plot, correcting most of my appalling spelling, and helping to bring my characters to life and, in particular, designing the splendid cover.

The mistakes and other matters of incompetence in this book are entirely my responsibility for which, dear Reader, I apologise.

G. de Gwymbach
Halkidiki, June 2024
gwymbach@lakescribe.com